HUG through Food

A Greek cook feeds American students

By Natasa Tsirmpa

Photographs by Nikias Alexandris

Cover Design by Vangelis Karakasis

Natasa and her husband studied in Chicago. He studied law at the University of Chicago and Natasa studied Interior Design at Columbia College. In 1992 they moved back to Greece with their first baby. In 2001, another move took them to France, this time with their three children. The three years of this rich cultural experience affected Natasa's understanding of food and enhanced her appreciation of the art of eating well. A few years later, Natasa decided to pursue another degree, and in 2019 she earned her MBA from Harding University.

Natasa was a stay at home mom for a period of about thirteen years, up until the youngest of their three children became seven years old. The decision to stay at home for those formative early years was a conscious choice the couple made in their desire for close family life. Together they created memories of long hours of play, reading, dancing, baking, of birthday parties full of magic and creativity and annual "chocolate days" -the French tradition on Saint Nicholas day-for their friends and the local church. When the time seemed ripe for her to re-engage with the professional world, Natasa worked in the financial department of a mid-size commercial and industrial company, from 2004 to 2013. Around that time an opportunity came up for her to become a professional cook and thus turn her hobby into her profession. She attended a private culinary school in the evenings while still keeping her day job. In January 2014 she started working as a cook for an American University that operates a study abroad program in Greece and she is still enjoying every minute of it!

Acknowledgments

I am deeply grateful to my husband and three children for supporting me in this crazy decision to leave a good and stable job and become a cook. They cheered me on every step of the way. On the first day of my job as a cook, after feeding 36 students for the first time, I came home to find Queen's song "We Are the Champions" blasting through the speakers! I would have never fulfilled my dreams of cooking professionally without my family's support!
They also helped me tremendously with the writing of this book, especially Natalie, who spent countless hours on this book.

I would like to thank my beloved aunt, Katerina Whitey, an author of many books, including the popular cookbook, *Around a Greek Table, Recipes and Stories*, who edited this book. My aunt and I share the love of cooking and hospitality.

I would also like to express my gratitude to Nikias Alexandris who took the cover photos and all of the artsy, really beautiful photographs in the book. The rest are mine.

I am very thankful for the work that Vangelis Karakasis put in designing the cover of this book. He is really an artist.

I want to thank Madeline Elliott, Hope Walker Smith, Miranda Farthing, Alexander Carlisle, Cassie Copeland and Emily Kymes who offered their time and expertise to help me.

I am deeply grateful to Mike and Beth James, the directors of the University program in Greece from 2010 to 2014, for taking a chance on me and making me a part of their study abroad program. Without them, I would have never even thought of getting involved with the program and with food professionally.

And lastly, I must thank the students who, over the course of these past seven years, have chosen to come to Greece for a semester, for their willingness and excitement to experience new flavors and textures. Because of them, I strive to become a better cook. Their contagious joy and love have made me excited to go to work every morning. And for that, I am deeply grateful!

My Instagram is natasa.alts. I would love to hear from you and answer any of your questions.

Introduction

Cooking is creative. Cooking is fun, rewarding and, yes, very time-consuming. Cooking is nurturing. Cooking is taking care of people and showing them love; showing them that we care. Our modern lifestyle convinced us that cooking is an inconvenience. We often opt for loopholes: frozen food, food delivery or eating out every day. I believe that these options have not enriched us as caregivers of our children and our loved ones. Instead, they have robbed us of the joy of creativity. We forgot the joy of sharing our love and showing how much we care for our families and for our friends through food. We are missing the opportunity to create a warm, inviting spot in our homes. We forgot what fun and how exciting hospitality can really be and how many precious memories can be made over a simple meal created with care. In the busy activities of daily living, we are missing the enticing aromas of slow-cooked food. Our kitchens have ceased to be the heart of the home and the place we gather to share our daily news with our family. I hope we grab the opportunity to reclaim the joy of nesting, of creating a safe, nurturing, and loving environment in our homes, where just being with our loved ones is enough. And enjoyable.

In Greek, the word for tasty is *νόστιμο* (nostimo). *Nostimo* shares the same etymological root as nostalgia (νοσταλγία), the heartache of missing home. The root is the ancient Greek word "nostos" which means homecoming. Let that sink in for a minute; the Greek language associates the concept of "tasty" with homecoming. Could it be that the flavors tasted in our childhood home get to define what tasty means for each one of us, as adults? We may walk away from those flavors and tastes at some point in our life, but they won't; they remain faithful to us, at times flooding us with memories and feelings when we least expect it to. The love our caregivers offered us was materialized in many ways and food was a very important one. This expression of love in the form of food we've received has shaped us in many and more profound ways than we often realize. Isn't that interesting? This idea awakens in me the desire to create good, nurturing food, not only for the body but also for the soul of the people I care about.

In this context, my aspiration is to contribute a little to an understanding of the creative techniques of cooking for young people. I hope that I will facilitate the awakening of that desire to create good food for their loved ones at home. As young people become adults, it is their turn to create new core groups, new families and new traditions. There is nothing more soothing and empowering than to return *home* to a safe, happy, inviting environment. Cooking is a big part of this homecoming.

Tips and Rules to help you become a better cook

1. It is important to buy good **quality ingredients** as the quality of your initial ingredients is sure to affect the flavor of the dish. If you use tasteless carrots, do not expect to make a tasty carrot cake. This kind of magic has not been invented yet.

2. When preparing a dish, try to be as **consistent** as possible with the size of the vegetables or meat you are cutting. Your food will taste better when the ingredients reach the various levels of the cooking process at the same time. This is partly due to the chemical reactions that take place during cooking (the technical name is a Maillard reaction). If such reactions happen simultaneously because the size is consistent, sugars are released at the same time and the food tastes better.

3. **Organize** yourselves. Some dishes require more time, others require last minute attention. Be mindful of the recipe and of any steps that are required, such as marinating your meat or letting your dough rise. Think ahead. Plan well. I plan my work while driving to work every morning, deciding in advance the order of my actions.

4. **Add ingredients carefully.** It is impossible to remove an ingredient that you have already added in your pot. It is very easy to add more. Be prudent when adding large quantities of a certain ingredient. Be particularly careful when adding water, since it can dilute the taste of what you are preparing very quickly.

5. **Taste.** Taste often and adjust the seasonings. I have a sign in my kitchen that reads "Never trust a skinny cook" (a gift from my dear sister-in-law). It's the cost cooks have to pay for making good food, as they constantly need to taste the food that is being prepared.

6. **Smell**. Be attentive to the smell when cooking. The moment your casserole or cake fills your kitchen with a "wholesome" aroma, the food is ready. What? You will know exactly what I am talking about when a symphony of fragrances wafts through the air. I still remember the first time I caught a whiff of the wholesome scent of my first broccoli soup in culinary school.

7. Invest in some **kitchen tools**. A good knife is a must. A mandoline, a scale, and a thermometer are necessary tools if you want to commit to cooking. A food processor, a mixer, or a hand blender are also extremely useful.

8. Cooking, like many skills, **takes time** to master. Do not get discouraged if you fail. You might make a certain dish very well and be extremely proud of it, only to prepare it a second time and be unsuccessful. Beginner's luck. Please do not give up. Did you stop driving when you scratched your car soon after getting your driver's license? Just keep cooking. You will get better and better. And cooking will only become more rewarding as time goes by.

9. **Follow the recipe**. It is important to follow the recipes without simplifying them, skipping or mixing steps, especially when you are new to cooking or when you are trying out recipes with which you are unfamiliar.

10. After you have practiced and honed your cooking skills, do not be afraid to become a little more creative and to **start experimenting** with recipes. I have made some of my best dishes after having deviated from a recipe or after having used a substitute when I am missing an ingredient. On the other hand, this food experimentation has also offered my children more than one funny story.

11. **Think and take notes** (mental or actual) of what you did differently than the recipe and how the dish turned out if it has turned out well. Then make the same dish again soon to solidify your technique. This is extremely important. This is how you master a dish.

12. Try to buy **fruit and vegetables that are in season**. No winter-grown tomato can ever be as flavorful as a summer-grown one. And while on the subject of tomatoes, try avoiding cans of tomato juice or sauce. I would advise you to opt for a glass container or a Tetra Pak. The lining of cans contains Bisphenol-A, which does not react well with the acidic tomatoes.

13. Every **oven is different**. Therefore temperature and time suggestions are just that: suggestions. Get to know "the personality" of your oven and adjust the baking time and temperatures accordingly.

14. The most important ingredient in baking desserts is **butter**. Every brand of butter offers a distinct flavor. Famous pastry shops use a certain brand of butter and do not deviate from it because the taste of their desserts will be affected. Find a good butter, one that you like and be consistent with using that butter.

This picture is from Emily Collier's Instagram account. Emily was a student in the spring semester of 2020.

Herbs and Spices

I never use premixed spices, whether they are called Italian spice mix, Greek, Mexican or other. These products do not enhance your cooking abilities, and may even steal your creativity. I would suggest trying to see what spices you like; start experimenting with spices and herbs one at a time, so that you can figure out what you like and what enhances the flavors of your dish. Try this, you will be surprised at the result. Apart from the delightful flavors, they add nutrients to your food. There are whole books on the health benefits of spices and herbs that ancient cultures knew- and used as medicine.

The flavor of fresh herbs is unparalleled. Fresh spearmint leaves add so much flavor and freshness in your burger patties. I understand that it may be difficult to keep fresh herbs all the time, so I always keep some dry ones in my cupboard because they too add flavor and depth in your dishes. Try to have a good variety of herbs and spices in your cupboard.

In general, we try to add the spices as early as possible, to let their aroma infuse the dish. When we make a meat stew, for example, we add the spices before any liquid, to let them heat up with the oil. The final flavor will be deeper. On the other hand, herbs should not be cooked for long periods of time because they lose intensity. Be especially mindful of the fresh herbs with green leaves (chlorophyll) because they turn bitter if cooked for more than thirty minutes.

Herbs: I always have oregano, thyme, spearmint, tarragon and rosemary. Spices: I always keep some cinnamon (preferably Ceylon cinnamon), cloves, paprika (sweet, spicy and smoked), peppercorn, cumin, turmeric, mustard powder, and whole nutmeg, that I like to grate on the spot. Freshly grated nutmeg, in my opinion, takes the dish up a notch. A lot of white preparations, i.e. Béchamel sauce, mashed potatoes, or chicken casserole, get an enticing aroma if nutmeg is added. And another piece of advice: invest in some good quality sea salt flakes. They add flavor, texture and so much interest to a dish. You cannot believe what a difference the right kind and amount of spices and herbs make in any dish and how different the taste will be if you use them instead of premixed spices.

Vegetable cuts

There are many YouTube videos on vegetable cuts. It is beneficial to watch some of them. It is even more beneficial to start practicing on cutting vegetables. It takes time to master but this process is a lot of fun.

These are the basic cuts:

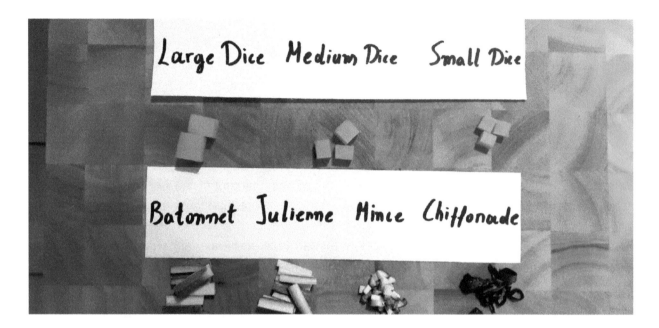

Large dice: 3/4 of an inch cubes
Medium dice: 1/2 of an inch cubes
Small dice: 1/4 of an inch cubes

Batonnet: 1/4 x 1/4 x 2 inches sticks
Julienne: match-size sticks
Mince: very fine cubes
Chiffonade: strings of herbs created by stacking leaves, rolling them tightly and then slicing them.

Useful Tools

From left to right:
A folding colander (very handy), a spray bottle (I use it ALL the time, I have one for water and one for oil), a hand blender, a cute tiny grater for nutmeg, a peeler, a garlic crush, an orange peeler, a chef's knife, a ceramic knife (good for potatoes and tomatoes), a cheese grater, a whisk, tongs, an apple corer, a metallic spatula, a rubber brush and a rubber spatula, an oven mitten.

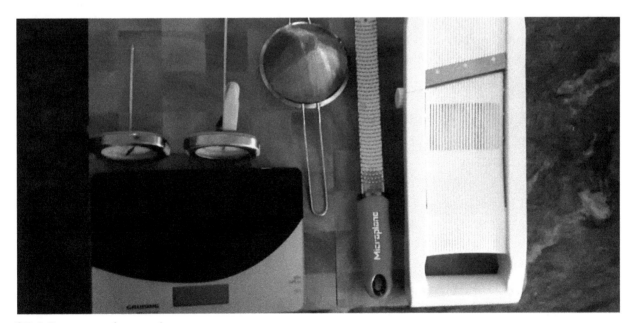

Slightly more advanced
From right to left: Two thermometers, the shorter one for meat and the bigger one for caramel (the two thermometers read different temperatures), a scale for precision in baking, a chinois strainer for soups or creams, a grater for citrus zest or cheese, a mandoline for vegetable cuts.

Helpful Cooking techniques used in this book

All recipes in this cookbook are for 4 to 6 people, except for the desserts, which are usually for 8 to 10 people.

It will be too cumbersome to list all cooking techniques here. There are many techniques I know but I have never used and even some others that I don't know at all. The ones I am including here are those I have used for recipes in this cookbook. The Greeks, being European, adapted many French terms in their cooking, so don't be surprised at the non-Greek sound of these words.

Bain Marie. When we want to melt chocolate or we need to cook eggs very gently so that they are pasteurized but do not become an omelet we use Bain Marie, also known as a water bath. We place our ingredients in a metallic bowl. We then place the bowl on top of a pot with simmering water and let the contents of the bowl cook for the needed amount of time. The bottom of the metallic bowl should not touch the simmering water at any point. The cooking or melting is achieved by steam.

Cheminée. This is a French word that simply means chimney. Take a parchment paper big enough to cover the top of your pot. Fold it in half, fold again twice, each time down the middle, in order to create a triangle (as shown in the first picture below). Place the folded paper above the pot, placing the center of the paper/corner of the triangle above the center of the pot and tracing with your finger or a pencil the edge of your pot, in order to measure its radius. Cut off a small part of the corner of the triangle as well as around the perimeter (across the line you traced in the previous step), to create a disc with a hole in the middle. (It sounds complicated but it is not). This is very handy when cooking and boiling vegetables. It prevents the boiling water from evaporating too quickly and helps keep the whole vegetable underwater. Also, after the heat has been turned off in a pot with meat, this method prevents the meat from turning dark.

The pictures will help you understand how to do this.

Gelatin. Before I went to cooking school, I would read a recipe and if it had the words "add gelatin", I would just skip the recipe altogether because I had no idea how to use it and it intimidated me. Gelatin is a transparent plastic-looking sheet or leaf. It is what we use at Christmas in the decoration of the Gingerbread houses as windows. If you add a gelatin sheet straight to your dessert, it will never dissolve. You simply have to accelerate the process of dissolving it, before you add it to your dessert or food. Therefore, when a recipe requires the use of a gelatin sheet, it should first be soaked in a bowl of cold water for 3-10 minutes. If you leave it for more than ten minutes it will start to dissolve. A few minutes after you place the gelatin sheets in the bowl of cold water, grab the wiggly and transparent sheets and pull them out of the water. Squeeze the excess water from the sheets and add them to the hot mixture that requires thickening. Make sure the mixture is no longer boiling, because the gelatin (which is collagen) may burn and leave an unpleasant taste if the temperature of the mixture is too high. Mix the gelatin well, and you are done. When the mixture cools off, the gelatin will thicken it up.

Dry Yeast. I have been baking since I was twelve years old. Until I went to culinary school (at the prime age of 44) I had never heard or read that salt kills dry yeast. This must be the best kept secret in baking. So, when making dough and you are using yeast, the first thing to do is to add the yeast to a liquid with sugar (which feeds the yeast), whether the liquid mandated by the recipe is water or milk. After this, you may add to the mixture half the flour mentioned in the recipe. Mix well. Add the other ingredients you are called to add, mix well, and *then* add the salt with the rest of the flour. This way, you won't run the risk of killing your yeast.

Bouquet Garni: This is simply a bunch of vegetables or herbs tied together with cooking twine to give a richer flavor to your food. The most common type is parsley stems (not leaves, they will become bitter when cooking for a long time), fresh or dry springs of thyme and a bay leaf to wrap around. You may also wrap the herbs in a cheesecloth. The one in the picture is a small bouquet of dry thyme, parsley stems and bay leaf, which can be used for a sautéed mushroom dish. When using the *bouquet garni* in a soup, or sauce, or stew, simply lift the *bouquet garni* up and discard before you serve.

Beurre Clarifié: means cleared butter which we achieve by burning the butter in a small pot. We end up with what the Asian Indians call ghee, and we have some amazing benefits. Firstly, by burning the butter, the milk protein (casein) is removed and lactose-intolerant people can eat it. Secondly, *beurre clarifié* has a higher burning point than butter. Therefore it is preferable to use *beurre clarifié* than butter when we want to fry meat or fish. Thirdly, *beurre clarifié* has a lovely nutty aroma and it enhances the flavor in desserts. I use it in my baklava. Fourthly, it lasts longer than butter when kept in the fridge.
You can make *beurre clarifié* by simply heating the butter up. There will be foam forming on the surface which you must remove with a slotted spoon. This is the casein. When a nutty aroma fills the kitchen and you start seeing burned particles on the bottom of the pot, remove it from the heat. Filter the burned butter through a fine strainer and you have the *beurre clarifié* that you can store in a clean jar. It is excellent.

SALADS: Greek salad

The Greek salad or Peasant salad, as the Greeks call it, is our summer salad. Since most tourists visit Greece in the summer months it has become widely known as the Greek salad. I will start with what ingredient the Greek salad does *not* have. And this is lettuce. There is also a big debate on whether the Greek salad should be dressed with vinegar or not. I do not add vinegar in my Greek salad, but you may do so. It will still be good. You can add as many or as few of the optional ingredients as you like.

2-3 red ripe tomatoes
1 cucumber
1/2 teaspoon salt
2-3 tablespoons extra virgin olive oil

Optional
100 grams feta cheese
Green, red and yellow peppers
1 red onion
10 Olives
1 teaspoon capers rinsed
1 scallion
Oregano or parsley
Croutons for crunchiness (they also absorb the tomato liquids and become extra tasty)

Wash the tomatoes, cucumber, and peppers well and cut the tomatoes first in half, and then each half in four or six pieces depending on the size of the tomato. Place them in a nice salad bowl. If the cucumber is organic, just cut it in wedges measuring a quarter of an inch. If it is not organic, peel it first. Add the cucumber to the bowl. Cut the green, red and yellow peppers in very thin slices. Cut the scallion lengthwise first and then in very thin slices. Rinse the capers. (Capers are packed with vitamins and are considered a superfood. Try to incorporate them in your diet). Add everything to the salad bowl. Then cut a red onion in thin slices and add it too. If you feel more adventurous, marinate the onion by doing this: peel the red onion and with a mandoline slice it very, very thin in a small bowl. Add two tablespoons of salt and make sure you mix the onion with the salt thoroughly with your fingers. This is an insane amount of salt, but it is used to marinate and take the heat off the onion. Let sit for 4-5 minutes and then squeeze the onion. A lot of juice will come out along with most of the salt. Place the onion in a strainer, rinse with water briefly and squeeze again. Add the rinsed onion to the salad, spreading it on top of all the other vegetables. Do not add more salt if you have marinated the onion. Add olive oil and oregano (if you wish). If you don't marinate the onion, add the salt first and the olive oil second. If you are adding feta, (which is very salty) be very careful with the amount of salt you add to the salad. Mix well and enjoy!

When to make this: right now!

Variation: Tabouli Salad

This is a very popular and very healthy salad in the Mediterranean diet. It is very easy to make; just be sure to let the bulgur soak in hot water for about an hour. I feel it is even better the day after you make the salad when the bulgur has marinated in the tomato juices. This salad stays good for two or three days in the fridge.

4 tablespoons bulgur
20 cherry tomatoes
2 cucumbers
2 scallions
1 red onion
1 cup of parsley
1 teaspoon salt
3 tablespoons olive oil
Juice of 1 lemon
1 tablespoon vinegar

Soak the bulgur in hot salted water for one hour. Drain. Cut the cherry tomatoes in half, the cucumbers in cubes, the scallions lengthwise first and then in very thin slices, dice the onion finely, and add them to a bowl together with the bulgur. Mince the parsley finely. We often tend to overminse our herbs. We have gone too far in minsing the herbs when we start seeing green juice on the cutting board because that is when we start losing flavor and vitamins. So, stop chopping the parsley as soon as you see green juice on your cutting board. Combine the parsley with the rest of the ingredients, add salt, olive oil, lemon juice and vinegar. Mix well and enjoy! I try to make this salad a couple of hours in advance to let the flavors infuse and the bulgur marinate in the salad juices.

When to make this salad: when you want something extremely easy, healthy and filling.

Winter salad

The traditional Greek salad for the winter season is a cabbage-based salad. It is packed with vitamin C, therefore ideal for the winter. This salad is best if made a few hours ahead of time.

Half a white cabbage
Half a small red cabbage
3 organic carrots
1 teaspoon salt
5 tablespoons olive oil
2 tablespoons red wine vinegar
2 tablespoons freshly squeezed lemon juice

Optional
Parsley
1/2 cup pomegranate seeds

Very thinly shred the cabbages. You can use a good knife or a mandolin to do this. You may also use a food processor, but do not overwork it. Grate the carrots in the food processor. Pulse the processor a few times, so that the carrots are not cut too thinly (they need to maintain some body). If you are adding parsley, chop it very thinly as well. If you want to add pomegranate seeds, cut a pomegranate in half, and with the help of a big sturdy spoon, beat the halved fruit several times. Beat the pomegranate with the cut side facing down, while holding it from underneath and over a bowl. Most seeds should come loose and fall. Repeat for the other half. The pomegranate will add beautiful color to the salad together with an interesting texture. It will also add a lot of vitamins. Mix all ingredients, add the salt, the olive oil, the vinegar and the lemon juice and taste. The olive oil should coat the salad well and the salad should have a very nice balance of salty and lemony flavors. If not, add more salt or lemon until this balance is achieved. It usually takes four or five adjustments for me to get it just right. Once you have this wonderful salty and lemony balance, let the salad rest and marinate outside of the fridge. It is best when consumed within three to five hours after you have made it. Refrigerate the salad if you are going to consume it after five hours from making it.

When using uncooked carrots, always prefer organic. All root vegetables (carrots, potatoes, radishes) collect and keep the pesticides used on them. Where potatoes are usually peeled and cooked, carrots are often consumed raw, so it is important to choose organic.

When to make this salad: when you feel that you need some color in your life.

Black-eyed pea salad

This is a wonderful salad that I like to serve with fish. Due to the amount of peppers in this salad, fish provides a good combination for nutritional reasons. Peppers, when served with fish, will help boost your immune system (and for the record, spinach also has the same nutritional benefits when paired with fish). Add or subtract any ingredients according to your palate. I used to call this salad "black-eyed beans" because we Greeks call them beans until I realized the students were laughing at me.

1/2 pound black-eyed peas
20 cherry tomatoes
1 cucumber
2 small carrots
1 yellow pepper
1 red pepper
1 green pepper
1 red onion
3 scallions
1 cup arugula
Parsley or cilantro (optional)
Salt
4-5 tablespoons olive oil
3-4 tablespoons red wine vinegar

Start by placing the black-eyed peas in plenty of cold water. Bring to a boil and then lower the heat. The peas should boil very gently for approximately thirty minutes or until they become tender, but take care to not let them become mushy. Drain and transfer them to a wide bowl, so that they cool faster on the large surface. Sprinkle with salt generously. Cut the cherry tomatoes in half. Cut the cucumber lengthwise twice (by making an X shape) and then cut perpendicularly in one inch chunks. Cut the carrots very thinly, in a julienne cut (see page 10). Cut all peppers into thin sticks. Cut all onions in very small dice (called a brunoise cut) and mince all greens. Add all vegetables to the cooled peas. Add 1 tablespoon salt, the olive oil and some vinegar. Mix well and taste. Adjust salt and vinegar, adding a little at a time until the taste of the salad is balanced. The taste should be "whole," filling your mouth with flavors. Adjusting the flavors is something you will be able to achieve with experience. But you have to start somewhere.

When to make this salad: when you have invited your parents over and you want to impress them with your maturity!

Oyster mushroom salad

This is a favorite salad with our students. If done well, it has a perfect balance of pepper and vinegar with a very strong Umami flavor. It might take you a couple of trials (or three) until you get it right, but it is worth the try. So, keep trying.

1 Romaine lettuce
Olive oil
1 package of oyster mushrooms (1/2 pound or 200 grams)
Five or six dry wild mushrooms (optional)
1/2 teaspoon salt
1 onion
Thyme, fresh or dry
Pepper
1 clove of garlic
2 tablespoons vinegar
1/2 cup of white cooking wine
1/2 cup heavy cream or
 Vegetable cream if you are vegetarian (make sure it is not sweet)

Wash the lettuce well. Drain it and cut it in small chunks with a knife. Set it aside.
Do *not* wash the mushrooms. Mushrooms are destroyed by water because they absorb it and then boil in it, losing all their flavor when our goal is to sauté them. There are ways to clean the mushrooms without washing them depending on the type. Oyster mushrooms are not cultivated on the ground and therefore there is not soil on them and do not need any washing or cleaning. Just cut the big chunky bases off and discharge them. Cut the rest of the mushroom in half inch cubes. Salt them and stir to mix. We want the salt to coat the surface of the mushrooms as much as possible. Place a heavy saucepan on high heat. Let it get really hot. Add 2 tablespoons of olive oil and when the oil is hot add the mushrooms. Cook stirring often until they start to darken. Dice one onion in small cubes and add to the pan. Cook for another 5 minutes. If there is no liquid left at this point add one more tablespoon of oil. Add thyme, preferably fresh, and lots of freshly ground pepper. Mix well. Add one clove of crushed garlic, wait until you can smell it (after around 30 seconds), and then add the vinegar. Mix again and add the wine. At this point add the dry mushrooms cut in small pieces, so that they regain moisture from the wine. When the mixture starts to boil (which means that the alcohol has evaporated) taste it. It should have a strong taste of vinegar and pepper, which is what we want because this taste will be counterbalanced by the cream. Let the mushrooms cook until the liquids are completely absorbed. Turn the heat down to the lowest possible level and add the cream. Let it cook for a couple of minutes, taste and turn the heat off. Adjust the taste adding salt or pepper. Let the mushrooms cool.
Place the lettuce in a bowl. Add a pinch of salt and 1 tablespoon of vinegar. Mix it well. Add the mushroom mixture on top. You can serve it with a nice steak and baked potatoes.

When to make it: when you invite your vegetarian friend. Make it when you invite your vegan friend, too, but make sure the vegetable cream is not sweet (some tend to be).

Poached pear salad

This is a fancy salad. Beautiful, tasty, and so worth the little extra time it takes.

1 Romaine lettuce
A handful of dried cranberries
1/2 pound or 200 grams of a soft goat cheese

2-3 pears
1 cup red cooking wine
2 tablespoons sugar

1/2 cup hazelnuts
1/2 cup almonds
3 tablespoons sugar
Salt

1/4 cup olive oil
2 tablespoons balsamic vinegar
1 teaspoon mustard
1 teaspoon honey

Start by peeling the pears. Cut them in halves and core them. Very carefully slice them so that you get about 6-8 slices from every half pear. Place all the slices in a small saucepan along with the wine and 2 tablespoons of sugar. The wine should cover the pear slices. Turn the heat on low, and simmer for fifteen minutes, or until the pears start to become translucent. They should be soft when you prick them. If the pears are still hard, let them simmer for five more minutes. Remove from heat and let them cool. You can prepare the pears 2-3 days in advance, take them out of the wine and keep them in an airtight container in the fridge.

In a heavy saucepan add the nuts and 2 tablespoons of sugar on medium heat. We want to roast them slightly to deepen their flavors and sweeten them, also slightly. The sugar/caramel should not coat them completely. This will take five to seven minutes. Do not leave the nuts unattended at all during this time. If you see that they start to darken, remove immediately.

Wash the lettuce well, drain and cut the leaves thin. Transfer to a nice serving bowl and add the cranberries and the goat cheese in clumps. Arrange the pears nicely and finally add the caramelized nuts. Sprinkle with 1/2 teaspoon salt and, just before serving, whisk up the olive oil, vinegar, mustard and honey until the mixture becomes a nice thick dressing. Taste and adjust the acidity or the sweetness of the dressing, if needed, so that it has a balanced taste and pour over the salad.

When I prepare this salad I make sure that I caramelize a lot more nuts than I need because students sneak into the kitchen and they just keep snacking on them. They are so good.

When to make it: when you invite me over. I can live on this salad.

Carrot salad

2 organic carrots
1 green apple
1 small swede or turnip
Half a fennel, root and stem
Half a pomegranate
Few walnuts
1/2 teaspoon salt
2 tablespoons olive oil

This winter salad will be a great addition to your Christmas table. It's refreshing, very tasty and beautiful to look at! Grate the carrots, cut one green apple in julienne cut (thin sticks as shown on 8) grate the swede (alternatively you can use turnips) and slice half a fennel very thinly on a mandoline. With a big spoon hit one half of a pomegranate over a bowl holding it with your other hand, cut side down. The seeds should come loose and fall in the bowl. Mix all ingredients and chop a handful of walnuts on top of the salad. Add two pinches of salt and two tablespoons of extra virgin olive oil.

When to make this: Christmas Eve, Christmas Dinner and every winter Sunday after that.

APPETIZERS

Greeks are very big on appetizers. It is not uncommon in Greece to go out with friends and eat nothing but appetizers. Nobody orders a dish for themselves, but they all order appetizers. We are talking about a lot of appetizers. It's fun because you get to try so many different tastes. In the end, you always end up with a fat, big, heavy stomach, but hey, you are in Greece. Enjoy life!

Here are some of the most popular appetizers. If you have ever visited Greece, you probably have already tasted them.

Shrimp with feta cheese, aka saganaki

This is a recipe that turns out great even if you use frozen shrimp.

1/2 pound fresh or frozen shrimp (if frozen let them thaw in the fridge, covered by a wet towel)
2-3 tablespoons olive oil
2 onions
1 green pepper
1 red pepper
1 carrot
1 clove of garlic
1 cup dry white wine
1/2 cup tomato juice
2 fresh tomatoes
5-6 ounces feta cheese
Freshly ground pepper
Parsley (optional)

Wash and cut your vegetables first. Slice the onion, cut the peppers in 1/4 inch slices and cut the carrot julienne (page 10). Crush the garlic. In a food processor puree the fresh tomatoes. If you prefer you can also dice them very small. Heat a heavy saucepan and add 2-3 tablespoons of olive oil. Add the onion and very little salt. Sauté for 3-4 minutes. Add the peppers and let them sauté for another couple of minutes. Add the carrot. Cook for another couple of minutes. By now the onions should be translucent and the aromas of the vegetables filling the kitchen. Add freshly ground pepper. Add the garlic and as soon as you can smell it (around thirty seconds) add the wine, tomato juice and pureed fresh tomato. Lower the heat and cook for 15 more minutes.

Turn the oven on at 380°F. By now some of the liquid should be absorbed, but there should still be some left in the pan. Add the shrimp and as soon as the liquid starts to boil again, turn the heat off. Transfer to a heatproof dish. Add the feta on top and place in the oven for about 20 minutes. Once the feta starts to melt, the dish is ready to be served. Sprinkle with minced parsley and serve with good bread. The sauce is delicious.

When to make this: when you want to feel you are in a Greek summer state of mind.

Yogurt dough cheese pie aka lazy person's pie

Here is *the* most popular cheese pie recipe with our students. It's also very easy to make. I have seen friendships go through a trial over the last remaining piece of this cheese pie. No matter how much I make, it is never enough. It is a baked pie, and because it requires a generous amount of olive oil it tastes as good as a fried one.

<u>Dough</u>
1 pound of Greek yogurt 2% or more. (You can use non-Greek yogurt, in which case you will need to add more flour because Greek yogurt is low in moisture.)
2.5 cups flour
2 teaspoons baking powder
3 tablespoons corn oil
A pinch of salt (very little)
2 tablespoons sugar
1 egg
1/2 pound or 200 grams yellow cheese, like gruyère. Mozzarella or Emmental also works well.

<u>Toppings</u>
10 ounces or 300 gr feta cheese
20 cherry tomatoes
Sea salt flakes
Red pepper flakes
Rosemary or Oregano
3/4 cup olive oil

Start by mixing the yogurt, half of the flour, the baking powder, the corn oil, the sugar and the egg with a whisk. If your yellow cheese is salty, do not add a pinch of salt in the dough. If it is not salty, add just a tiny bit. Slowly add the rest of the flour, mixing by hand to create a soft dough. It should be very soft, almost sticky (it might need more or less than 2.5 cups flour depending on the moisture of the yogurt). Lastly, add the yellow cheese. Turn the oven on at 420°F. In an 8 x 12 ceramic or Pyrex dish add 1/2 a cup of olive oil. I know it is a lot, but it is all going to be absorbed by the dough. Add the dough in the pan, and spread as evenly as possible with your fingers. It should be about an inch thick, or a little more. Crumble the feta cheese on top and press with your palms, so that the feta cheese becomes almost embedded in the dough. We don't want it sticking out too much because it will burn. Add the rest of the olive oil (1/4 cup) on top. Slice the cherry tomatoes in half and place them on the dough. Sprinkle the dough with sea salt flakes, red pepper flakes, chopped rosemary or oregano. Bake for 50 minutes or until the bottom of the pie is very well baked, but not burned.

One of our students once spread the rumor that I made this weird cheese pie with raspberries, in hopes that he would gross everyone out. It did not work.

When to make this: when your best friend is coming over and all you want to do is talk and snack all day.

Fried cheese pie from Alonissos

Alonissos is a stunning island, really beautiful, with wonderful beaches and the best fried cheese pie. You need to make your own dough to make this pie. I know it sounds intimidating but if you think about it, for thousands of years in human history people have been making their own dough, so I say you give it a try.

In Alonissos the cheese pie is made with feta cheese. The islanders also make a sweet version of this fried beauty with apple, sugar and cinnamon. If you want to make this, just cut the apple in small pieces.

<u>Dough</u>
1 cup water
A pinch of salt
2 tablespoons of olive oil
1 teaspoon red wine vinegar
2.5 to 3 cups flour
3/4 pound or 350 grams feta cheese
Corn oil for frying (or any other oil)

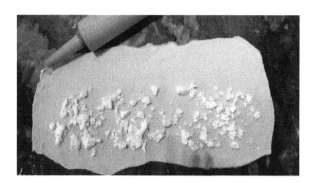

Start by mixing all dough ingredients except for the flour. Slowly add the flour, a little at a time. Knead the dough and stop adding flour as soon as the dough is no longer sticky, but still soft. It should take around 2.5 cups. Knead for 4-5 minutes, pressing the dough with your palm, pushing it away from you, folding it in on itself and then turning it 45 degrees. Do this in a rhythmic motion. You will find that it is quite

enjoyable, almost therapeutic. If it starts to stick, dust it with flour. Cover it up with a bowl and let it rest for at least 30 minutes. Cut the dough and form three balls. With a rolling pin (hope you have one) start opening up one dough ball by pressing the rolling pin from the middle of the dough and away from you. Turn the dough 45 degrees and do it again, repeating many times until your dough is very thin, almost translucent. We want to end up with roughly a rectangular dough, where the long side is three times longer than the short side. Break the feta cheese in clumps, sprinkle on top of the dough, leaving a long strip of dough without cheese and roll the dough over itself (the longer side of the dough should be the length of your pie). Pinch each end of your cheese pie to close it. Make a snail shape and fry in one inch deep preheated oil, in medium heat. If the heat is too high, the outside of your dough will burn while the inside will stay raw, and if the heat is too low the dough will absorb more oil than we want by the time it is ready. Repeat the process with the remaining dough or make an apple pie with sugar and cinnamon stuffing instead of feta. Serve immediately.

I hope you give it a try. It's so worth it.

When to make it: when you're hungry and also feel like giving your triceps a workout.

Cheese pie pockets with honey and sesame

This cheese pie is absolutely delicious. You will need as many phyllo dough sheets as your guests and as many feta cheese slices. The feta cheese should be around 2 x 3 inches, with half an inch thickness. I have to confess that this is a recipe that I do not make when we have big groups. It is kind of impossible to fry fifty of these, even in a professional, state-of-the-art kitchen like the one we have at school.

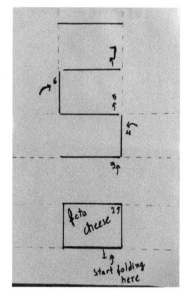

4 phyllo dough sheets
4 blocks of feta cheese
4 tablespoons honey
4 teaspoon sesame seeds

Place one cheese block on a phyllo sheet. Wrap it very carefully, folding it according to the picture, so that the cheese is completely enclosed. Repeat until all cheese blocks are wrapped in phyllo. Place on a plate, so that the cheese "pockets" are not touching each other and wrap them in plastic wrap and refrigerate for at least 15 minutes, or place in the freezer for no longer than 10 minutes. Just before you are ready to eat, fry them in vegetable oil over medium heat. Place the "pocket" with the last fold of the phyllo facing down in the frying pan. If you place the last fold facing up it will just puff open when it starts to fry. Fry on both sides until the color is golden brown. Once you have removed each "pocket" from the pan, drizzle with honey and sprinkle a few sesame seeds on top. Enjoy your cheese pies and the wonderful combination of the sweet honey with the salty feta cheese.

When to make it: when you're craving something sweet, salty, crunchy, soft and chewy, or just simply, all of the above!

Kataifi phyllo cheese pie

Kataifi phyllo is a dough that looks like very fine strings of dough or shredded dough. It is made by allowing the watery dough to run through small slots on a heated surface that spins, thus creating long, very thin threads of dough. It is wonderful because it absorbs butter or syrup when baked and it becomes very fluffy (if you use butter) or crunchy (if you use syrup) and tasty. I believe you can find it frozen in Middle Eastern markets and some supermarkets, especially near Christmas time. If you find it, try to make this cheese pie.

The comment that I usually get for this pie is that it is goodness in a cotton texture. It's airy, it's yummy and it melts in your mouth.

One stick of unsalted butter, melted
One package of kataifi dough defrosted (about 400 grams)
7 ounces or 200 grams feta cheese
7 ounces or 200 grams mozzarella or another non salty cheese (Gouda works well)
3 eggs
1 cup half and half cream
Freshly ground pepper
Freshly ground nutmeg

Butter an 8 x 12 Pyrex pan. Place and spread half of the dough in the buttered pan. If the kataifi dough strings are stuck together, divide into small portions and rub between your palms, as if you want to form the dough into a ball. The strings will come apart ensuring a fluffy final outcome. Drizzle with half the butter. Spread the feta cheese in crumbles and then the mozzarella. Add the rest of the dough on top and press with your palms lightly. Pour the rest of the butter over the cheese pie. In a small bowl combine the eggs and cream with the pepper and nutmeg (nutmeg is a wonderful spice and is very fragrant when it is freshly ground). Pour slowly over the cheese pie, making sure you have moistened the top surface as much as possible. Let the pie sit and absorb the liquid for 15-20 minutes. Turn the oven on at 400°F degrees and bake until golden. Eat warm.

When to make it: whenever you manage to get your hands on kataifi phyllo!

Soufflé

"A soufflé never waits for the guests, the guests wait for the soufflé!" - French saying.

Soufflés are delectable, fluffy and overall wonderful! The reason I love soufflés is that you can choose almost any base ingredient and end up with something delicious, whether it's sweet or savory.

A soufflé is made of three components: a cream sauce, usually béchamel; eggs, separated into yolks and whites, which have been whipped; and of course, your ingredient of choice. They are wrongly perceived as very difficult to make. All you need to do is master the folding of whipped egg whites or meringue (as egg whites are called when sugar has been added) into the sauce and voilà! Your soufflé is ready! Well, not really, but almost.

My personal favorite is an orange soufflé and my husband's is the spinach soufflé. So, start experimenting until you find your favorite one!

Spinach soufflé

4 tablespoons butter (plus a little more for the dish)
6 tablespoons flour
3 cups milk
1 cup of frozen spinach thawed
1/2 cup grated Emmental (optional)
Salt
3 egg yolks + 3 egg whites at room temperature

In a heavy saucepan over medium heat melt four tablespoons of butter. Add the flour, stirring constantly and cook for 2 minutes. Gradually add the milk in the mixture while whisking. Lower the heat and continue whisking while the mixture thickens up. It will turn into a nice thick and smooth sauce. At this point taste the sauce. If you can still taste the flour, cook while stirring constantly for a couple more minutes. You might need to add half a cup more milk if the sauce becomes too thick. Squeeze the thawed spinach to remove as much moisture as possible. Add the spinach, salt and the 3 egg yolks to the saucepan and mix well. If you want to use cheese, add it now. Be sure to taste at this point. Be very careful with salt and spinach. One minute it is salt-free and half a teaspoon of salt later, it becomes too salty. Be careful. Preheat the oven at 380°F if you are using ramekins or at 400°F degrees if you are using a soufflé baking pan (they have high straight sides). If you don't have one, it's not the end of the world; just use one that has relatively high sides. Butter your baking pan. Whip the egg whites (they should be at room temperature) with a hand blender or a mixer until the mixer whisk leaves a noticeable trail on the egg whites. With a spatula start incorporating the beaten egg whites into the spinach mixture, in batches- 1/3 in the beginning- so that the mixture becomes lighter. Once you have incorporated the first 1/3, add the rest and fold. Your movement should be soft and slow and steady. Fold the mixture gently with your right hand in a semicircular motion from top to bottom, while at the same time turning the bowl counterclockwise with your left hand. Pretend that there is a small balloon in there; you want to trace it, but you don't want to break it. After about ten strokes, the mixture should be ready, with no visible white lumps. Transfer to the baking pan, level the top and bake for around 50 minutes, without opening the oven. Towards the end, you can open the oven, check that the soufflé is not wiggly and serve immediately!

Cheese soufflé

4 tablespoons unsalted butter (plus a little for the pan)
6 tablespoons flour
3 cups milk
Pepper
Freshly ground nutmeg
3 ounces grated gouda cheese
3 ounces grated edam
3 ounces grated Emmental
3 ounces grated pecorino Romano
3 ounces grated gruyère
3 egg yolks
3 egg whites (room temperature)
You could use 10 ounces of gouda or Emmental and skip the rest of the cheeses, but the variety creates a more flavorful and rich soufflé.

In a heavy saucepan over medium heat melt four tablespoons of butter. Add the flour, stirring constantly for a couple of minutes and then slowly start adding the milk in the mixture. Lower the heat and continue whisking while you gradually incorporate the milk. It will become a nice thick, smooth sauce. At this point, you can taste the sauce. If you can still taste the flour, cook while stirring for a couple more minutes. You might need to add half a cup more milk if the sauce is too thick. This sauce is called béchamel. Let cool, preferably completely. If you add the cheeses while the cream is still hot, the soufflé will not be as fluffy as if you add them after the cream has completely cooled down.
Preheat the oven at 400°F degrees and butter a soufflé baking pan (it should be tall with straight walls). Add pepper and nutmeg. Add the egg yolks and a cup and a half of the cheese mixture and mix. Whip the egg whites until the peaks are soft when you lift the mixer whisk. We do not want to over beat the egg whites to the point that the peaks are stiff. Mix a little of the egg whites in the soufflé with soft movements to loosen the mixture up and then mix in the rest of the egg whites. Your movement should be soft and slow and steady. With your right hand fold the mixture gently in a semicircular motion from top to bottom, while at the same time turning the bowl counterclockwise with your left hand. Pretend that there is a small balloon in there; you want to trace it, but you don't want to break it. When all the egg white mixture is incorporated, transfer to the pan and bake for 50 minutes (without opening the oven) until a nice golden color has been achieved. Towards the end, you can check that the soufflé is not wiggly. Serve immediately.

These five kinds of cheese are an excellent combination. I often buy them, mix them up and use them together. They balance and enhance each other in a great way. You can save the unused portion in a big ziplock. I even freeze them, grated. Since they are all cheeses with very little moisture, they come out of the freezer in excellent condition. Try to push as much air out of the bag as possible before you close it. They are also perfect for a grilled cheese sandwich.

When to make a soufflé: on a Sunday or at a celebration of any kind. Any meal becomes a celebration with a soufflé!

VEGETABLES

When you make a vegetable dish, always remember that the final taste will be impacted by the initial quality of your vegetables, which depends on various parameters (i.e. whether they are organic or not and whether they have been harvested prematurely or not). Vegetables that have been harvested at the right time, that is, left to mature on the plant, cannot be compared in taste to the ones we find at the supermarkets, which have matured on the way to the supermarket shelves. You can find a lot of great products at Farmers Markets. It might be time consuming to shop there but the quality and the taste of their products are definitely worth the extra effort. This is a zucchini flower.

Grilled peppers and feta

Six green peppers (jalapenos or *pimentos de Padrón*)
2 tablespoons olive oil
1 tablespoon balsamic vinegar
A pinch of salt
Red pepper flakes
1 tomato
2 scallions
1 tablespoon olive oil
5 ounces or 150 grams feta cheese

You can use any pepper that is good for roasting. Wash the peppers, take off the top and rinse the seeds away. After rinsing them, shake off the excess water. Cut them in 1/4 inch thick rings and place them in a casserole dish. Turn on the broiler in your oven. Drizzle the peppers with 2 tablespoons olive oil, 1 tablespoon of balsamic vinegar, a pinch of salt and the red pepper flakes, and let them marinate for five to ten minutes. Place the dish in the oven under the broiler, on the second lowest rack. Meanwhile, place the tomato, scallions, parsley and 1 tablespoon olive oil in a food processor and pulse for a few seconds to make the salsa. The peppers should start to brown in 5-6 minutes. Remove the dish, add the salsa and the feta cheese in crumbles on the peppers and return the dish to the oven. Bake for another 5 minutes and then turn the oven off. The peppers and the feta should have softened nicely and have a nice golden brown color. If not, just leave the pan in the oven with the heat off for a few more minutes.

When to make it: when you are planing to deep clean your house. You can snack on something easy, filling and rewarding all day.

Fried Zucchini

Fried zucchini is a Greek classic and our students' favorite vegetable dish.

4 medium-sized zucchinis

2 cups cold beer (you may use a can of 500 ml or 17 ounces)

2 cups and 2 tablespoons flour (depending on the humidity, it might take 1 or 2 tablespoons)

1/2 teaspoon salt

2 teaspoon baking powder

Vegetable oil for frying

Wash each zucchini and cut the hairy top off. With a mandoline, slice them a little thinner than 1/4 of an inch thick. Place a clean kitchen towel on a flat surface and arrange all zucchini slices in a single layer. We want the zucchinis' surface to dry as much as possible; otherwise, it will not become crispy when we fry it. The slices should be dry in about 30 minutes if the room is well ventilated. Right before you are ready to serve, preheat a frying pan and prepare the batter. Mix the cold beer with the flour, the salt, and the baking powder. The mixture should coat your zucchini slices well and stick to them. Start dipping them in the batter and VERY carefully dropping them in the heated oil one at a time, so that the slices do not stick together. When the batter covering the zucchinis turns into a golden crust, remove them with a slotted ladle and place them on a platter lined with paper towels, so that the excess oil is absorbed, and your vegetables stay crispy. Replace the paper towels as often as you need. Fry the zucchini slices in batches and do not overcrowd the frying pan. Placing too many zucchinis in the pan will cause the temperature to drop too much, the zucchinis will absorb too much oil and you will end up with soggy fried zucchini.

Tzatziki Sauce

If you order fried zucchini in Greece, you have to order tzatziki sauce with it. These two go together. The basic ingredient is yogurt, so you have to choose your yogurt carefully. Do not use a 0% yogurt. Use the Greek FAGE or Greek Gods yogurt for a nice texture. Now Greeks want their tzatziki thick with very little moisture, but the truth is that it's not the end of the world if your tzatziki sauce is thinner. The taste will be just as good.

1 pound yogurt 2% or 5%
2 tablespoons olive oil
1 tablespoon red wine vinegar
1 clove garlic, crushed
1/2 cucumber
1 teaspoon salt, pepper
Optional: dill, finely minced

Wash the cucumber and grate it. Squeeze it to discard the excess juice (remember the Greeks want the Tzatziki sauce to be thick, not watery). Add the squeezed, grated cucumber to the yogurt along with the crushed garlic and the rest of the ingredients. Mix well and refrigerate for at least thirty minutes.
Dill will give it a distinct freshness, but be careful with it since a lot of people feel that its taste is too strong.

Raw zucchini marinated

This is an interesting recipe that has been received with enthusiasm by our students. I was hesitant to serve this dish to 20-year-olds, but I was wrong. Make sure your zucchini is organic and very fresh.

6 small zucchinis (the smaller the better, because they will be more tender)
1/4 cup olive oil
3 tablespoons red wine vinegar
1 clove of garlic crushed
1 red onion minced
1/2 teaspoon oregano
Fresh pepper
1 teaspoon salt

Add all ingredients, except for the zucchini, in a glass bowl and mix well.
Wash the zucchinis and cut the tops off. Julienne them, as shown on page 10. Alternatively, you could slice the zucchinis on your mandoline if it has a julienne setting (small blades that are perpendicular to the big horizontal one). Add the julienned zucchini to the glass bowl and mix carefully. Cover with saran wrap and place in the fridge for at least 12 hours, or overnight. You may serve the zucchini as it is. You can also drain the olive oil before you serve it, but if you do so, don't throw away the olive oil just yet. This very aromatic olive oil can be drizzled on slices of toasted bread or, even better, drizzled on bread and then toasted. This bread will go wonderfully with the zucchini.

When to make this: When you have your raw-vegan friends over. They will love it.

Zucchini patties

This recipe is one of my favorites. It is an easy recipe, but there is one catch; you have to grate the zucchinis and let them drain for at least 30 minutes; otherwise, the patties will be too moist, to the point that you may not even be able to form and fry them.

5 zucchinis
1 tablespoon salt to marinate the zucchini
1 big carrot
1 red onion
1 cup flour
1 teaspoon baking powder
1 egg
1 tablespoon fresh peppermint (optional)
1/2 cup cheese (you can use feta cheese or yellow cheese, like Emmental)
1/2 teaspoon salt
Pepper to taste
Olive oil or vegetable oil for frying

Grate the zucchini. You may use your food processor if it has an attachment for grating. Place the zucchini in a colander, add one tablespoon salt and mix well with your fingers so that the salt coats the zucchini. Leave the zucchini there for at least 30 minutes, massaging it every ten minutes or so. In the meanwhile, grate the carrot, mince the onion and add the rest of the ingredients to a bowl. Work the zucchini again with your fingers and squeeze it as much as possible to remove the excess juices. Then, add it to the rest of the ingredients and form into small patties.

Place a heavy saucepan on medium heat, add oil, about half an inch deep, and once the oil has been heated thoroughly, start forming the patties into disks with your palms and frying them. They should not be placed too close to one another, to avoid a sudden temperature drop in the pan. Check their color after four or five minutes and if they are golden brown flip the patties over and fry them on the other side as well. After each batch of patties is ready, remove from the saucepan and place them on kitchen paper to drain the excess oil. Eat warm!

When to make it: when your vegetarian friend is coming over but you still want to have a burger (you may skip the egg and the cheese in the recipe).

Vegetable patties: Cauliflower

Similar to the zucchini patties, there are many vegetable-based pattie recipes. They all follow the pattern - vegetable, carrot, onion, egg, flour and, optionally, cheese. A big hit with our students is the cauliflower patties. We had a student once who had assured me that he would never, ever, try cauliflower. When I made the cauliflower patties he devoured them, without exactly knowing what he was eating….oops.

2 cups cauliflower chopped in the food processor
1 carrot
1 red onion
1 teaspoon parsley or peppermint
1 egg
1 cup flour
1 teaspoon baking powder
Salt
Pepper
1/2 cup milk
1/2 cup feta cheese (optional)

<u>For the salsa</u>
1 ripe tomato
1 small onion or scallion
1/2 green pepper
1 tablespoon parsley
Salt to taste
1 tablespoon olive oil
Tabasco sauce to taste

Chop the cauliflower in the food processor until it resembles coarse sand. Do not overwork it. Probably five or six pulses will be enough. Chop the carrot in the food processor as well, but mince the onion by hand (the food processor tends to mince onions too much, making them lose all their juice and flavor). Add all ingredients in a bowl, and crumble in the feta cheese. Mix well. Deep fry the patties by dropping a tablespoon of the mixture in hot oil, very carefully. Keep a cup of water nearby to dip in the spoon every time it becomes sticky. Do not overcrowd the fryer. When nice and golden, take out with a slotted ladle and drain them on a platter lined with kitchen paper towels. You can also make them without the feta cheese. They are still very nice.
I like to serve them with fresh salsa. Add all the salsa ingredients to a food processor and work until all are chopped. Add as much Tabasco sauce as you like, and serve.

When to make them: when you have a barbecue party. Serve with salsa and chips. They will be a hit. Don't forget to double or triple the recipe.

Sautéed Vegetables

A wonderful way to consume vegetables is to *sauté* them. By wonderful, I mean easy, healthy, yummy. You can *sauté* cauliflower, broccoli, green beans, carrots, leeks, pumpkins or squash to name just a few. In the spring, asparagus is the absolute sautéed vegetable star. Sautéed spinach is also very tasteful and makes an elegant side dish. The technique goes like this:

1. ***Blanché* the vegetable**: immerse the vegetable into salted boiling water, very briefly, depending on the size of the vegetable. Immerse spinach for 30 seconds, asparagus for two minutes, carrot for one. Take them out with a slotted ladle and
2. **bring their cooking to a halt** by plunging the vegetable into an ice bath (a bowl of water with ice). When completely cool remove the vegetables and place them on a kitchen towel to drain. (This is the best point to freeze the vegetables if you wish because the enzymes that cause the growth and maturity of the vegetables have been neutralized in the blanching process).
3. ***Sauté*** them in olive oil until their skin turns into a nice deep golden color.

To give an example, I will describe how to *sautée* a cauliflower.

Wash the cauliflower and remove the outer leaves. Bring 2 quarts of water with one tablespoon of salt to a soft boil. Add the cauliflower, with the core of the cauliflower being at the bottom. Let it boil for about 7-8 minutes. Remove from the pot with a slotted spoon and immerse in a bowl of ice water to stop the cauliflower's cooking. When completely cool (for a medium cauliflower that would be three minutes), remove it from the water and place it on kitchen paper to dry. Leave it on the paper for a few minutes. Slice it in three or four big slices (depending on the size of the cauliflower). Make sure you use a big knife to create clean slices to facilitate the next step. In a heavy saucepan add two tablespoons of olive oil. When the oil is hot add the cauliflower slices. If the cut is clean and the surface of the slice is flat, the browning of the vegetable will be more homogenous. Sprinkle the cauliflower slices with salt, pepper and paprika. Turn both sides until a nice, slightly brown color is achieved. This way of cooking brings out the flavors of the vegetable in the best way. If you are using a smaller vegetable, like a carrot, for example, immerse in the boiling water for only 1 minute.

I understand that step 2 might seem too complicated or extreme to some. I would rather have you try the sautéed vegetables while skipping step 2, than being intimidated out of trying to make them altogether. Therefore, if you are to skip step two, just leave the vegetable in the boiling water for a shorter time. Take them out thirty seconds earlier and let them dry on a kitchen paper before you sauté them.

If you want to sauté spinach, immerse the leaves in the simmering water and remove them almost immediately. Drain the leaves very well and then sauté them in olive oil for a few minutes. You can finish the spinach dish off by adding half a cup of heavy cream on very low heat for one minute. This elegant side dish will enhance your main dish, whether it is meat or fish (I particularly recommend the latter for nutritional reasons).

When to make sautéed vegetables: probably every day. God has blessed us with such a variety of vegetables, flavors and textures, but we limit ourselves to eating the same three vegetables over and over again. Experiment and choose a different one each week.

Sautéed mushrooms

1 package mushrooms
3-4 tablespoons olive oil
1/2 teaspoon thyme
Pepper
1 red onion
1 clove garlic
1/2 cup red or white wine
1/2 cup heavy cream (optional)

Here you can see a half-way peeled mushroom, the peels that are to be thrown away and a sliced mushroom that is ready to be used.

Mushrooms are fungi but for all practical purposes can be cooked and used as vegetables, with small adjustments to fit their unique attributes. Mushrooms cannot be sauteed as described in the previous recipe because water ruins them. Mushrooms do not need to be washed if bought from the supermarket. They are cultivated either indoors or in an enclosed area, and all you need to do is to remove any visible dirt with a brush or a damp paper towel. I peel them in case there is any dirt on top, but I know many chefs who don't. Remove the stem, and cut off and discharge the very bottom half inch. Put the rest of the stem in a bowl. With one hand keep the mushroom top side down and with the other hand start peeling it, as shown in the picture. Slice the mushroom or cut it in four pieces, if it is a small one. After you have cleaned and cut all of your mushrooms, sprinkle them with a generous pinch of salt and mix them around. Set a heavy saucepan on very high heat and as soon as it becomes very hot, place the mushrooms in a single layer covering the bottom of the saucepan. We want the initial heat shock to be as intense as possible. Do not overcrowd the saucepan. It's better to cook them in two or more batches, if necessary. Stir the salted mushrooms for one minute in the saucepan, and then add 2 tablespoons olive oil. The mushrooms should now start cooking/frying. Let them cook for a couple more minutes, stirring once or twice. By now the mushrooms will have browned. Add thyme and pepper. Add the onion in nice thin slices. Cook with the onion for 3-4 minutes. Crush in the garlic and let it cook for only thirty seconds. Be very careful with the garlic because if you burn it, it will become bitter. If you have a second batch to cook, take out the first batch, transfer to a clean bowl and repeat the process with the second batch. After you have added the garlic and cooked it for thirty seconds on the last batch, transfer all mushrooms back to the saucepan and add the wine. When all the wine has evaporated you can add the cream. At this point, turn the heat to the lowest possible degree and cook for one more minute, so that your cream does not curdle. I like to use cream with white wine but not with red because the taste of red is usually fuller.

Leek soup

Leek is very widely used in Greece and for a good reason. It is healthy and brings with it a welcoming sweetness.

4 tablespoons olive oil
1 tablespoon salt
1 onion
1 carrot
1 celery
4 big leeks or six small ones
2 potatoes
1/2 cup of white wine (optional)
1 cup chicken broth
5 cups water
1/2 cup cream
1 tablespoon flour
For garnish
Pepper
Goat cheese
Parsley

Peel the onion, the carrot and the potatoes and cut them in big dice, along with the celery, and set aside. Wash the leeks and cut the roots off as close to the end as possible. The white section is the sweetest part of the vegetable. Cut the dark green part off and remove the exterior leaf. If you see brown stuff between the rings, this is soil and it should be removed. Cut a little bit more off and wash it. Slice the rest of the leeks in quarter inch thick rings.

Place a big pot on high heat, and add 4 tablespoons of olive oil. Add the onion, carrot, celery and a pinch of salt. Five minutes later add the leeks and stir. Cook for another 3 minutes and add the potatoes. Continue cooking, stirring often for another 3 minutes, and then add the white wine, the chicken broth and 5 cups of water. With a wooden spatula scrape the bottom of the pot to make sure that no burned sugars remain stuck. Let the soup come to a boil and then turn the heat on low. Add salt and pepper and taste. Let the soup simmer for thirty minutes. At this point, the soup should smell and taste really good. Give it another five minutes if you feel that the taste is not full yet. Use a hand blender or any other blending tool you have to purée the vegetables found in the soup. Consistency is very important. If the soup is too thick, add some more water. One cup is fine but if you need more liquid, add chicken broth to avoid diluting the taste with too much water. Add one tablespoon of flour to the cream (if the soup is too thin add two tablespoons of flour), mix well and add to the soup. Let it come to a simmer again and then turn the heat off. Taste again and adjust the salt. Serve hot with a piece of good goat cheese in it. The cheese will melt in the hot soup and it will be exquisite.

It's always interesting to see the students' expressions as they are just about to try their first spoonful of leek soup. Terrified! And then, just like that, the soup is gone.

When to make it: when you want a fancy dinner.

Potato soup

This is similar to the leek soup. Just replace the leeks with potatoes, add some bacon and you have a delicious potato soup.

4 tablespoons olive oil
4 slices of bacon
salt
1 onion
1 carrot
1 celery
1 big leek
4 potatoes
1/2 cup of white wine (optional)
1 cup chicken broth
6 cups water
1/2 cup milk or cream
1 tablespoon flour
<u>For garnish</u>
Pepper
Parsley
Red pepper flakes

Peel and cut the onion, the carrot, the celery and the potatoes in big dice and set aside. Cut the root of the leek and the top dark green part off. Pay attention to the green part to see if there is any soil. You will see brown stuff between the rings if there is soil. Cut a little bit more off and wash it. Do not throw it away. Slice the leeks in quarter inch thick rings.

Place a big pot on medium heat, and add the olive oil. Add the bacon in small slices and fry until light brown. Remove as much of the bacon as you can, and do not worry about any pieces stuck to the bottom of the pot. Turn the heat on high and add the onion, the carrot, the celery and a pinch of salt. Three minutes later add the leek and stir. Cook for another 2-3 minutes and add the potatoes, stirring often for another 3 minutes. Add the white wine, the chicken broth and 6 cups of water. With a wooden spatula scrape the bottom of the pot to make sure that no burned sugars remain stuck there. Bring to a boil and then turn the heat on low. Taste and add salt and pepper. Let it simmer for thirty minutes. Use a hand blender or any other blending tool you have to purée the soup. If you have one of those conical sieves, called chinois, run the soup through it. The texture will be silky and wonderful. The consistency of the soup is very important. If the soup is too thick, add some more water. One cup is fine but if you need more liquid, add chicken broth to avoid diluting the taste with too much water. If the soup is too thin add one or two tablespoons of flour to the milk or cream, mix it well and add it to the soup. Bring to a boil and then turn the heat off. Taste again for salt and pepper. You can toast some good bread if you like to serve with the hot soup.

When to make it: on a rainy weekday.

Spinach Rice

Spinach rice is a surprisingly delicious dish. For Greeks, a plate of spinach rice with a slice of feta cheese and a couple of slices of good bread is an ideal lunch. It is extremely quick to make, easy and so healthy!

1 pound of spinach
4 tablespoons olive oil
1 big red onion
3 scallions
1 cup of long-grain rice
1/2 cup freshly squeezed orange juice
1/4 cup freshly squeezed lemon juice

Wash the spinach and drain it in a colander. If you're in a rush, with the help of some kitchen paper, pat it dry for 10-15 seconds. We want as little water as possible because we want to sauté it. In a heavy saucepan add the olive oil, the onion minced, the white part of the scallion, and a pinch of salt. Cook on medium heat for 3-4 minutes. Add a third of the spinach and stir until it loses its volume. Add the second third and stir until the loss of volume, and then the third. You should have added all the spinach in about three minutes. Add the green part of the scallions, the rice, one cup and a half of water, as well as half a teaspoon of salt. Stir and turn the heat down to low. Let the spinach rice cook for ten minutes. In ten minutes most of the water should have evaporated and the rice should be almost, but not completely ready yet. Taste a grain of the rice to make sure that it is almost done. If not, add half a cup of water and wait for two more minutes. Add the fresh orange juice and lemon juice, turn the heat off and cover with a kitchen towel. Leave the pot with the spinach rice on the hot stove, so that the juices are absorbed and the steam in the pot completes the rice's cooking.

You can eat it warm or at room temperature and pair it with a variety of side dishes. You can try it with feta cheese, a few cherry tomatoes, drizzled with a bit of olive oil, or couple it with a grilled cheese sandwich or serve it with smoked salmon. And these are just a few of your options!

When to make it: when you want to eat something exotic but you only have fifteen minutes to make dinner.

Spinach Tart

<u>For the dough</u>
125 grams or 1 cup flour
60 grams or 1/2 stick butter
15 grams or 1 tablespoon sugar
3 grams or 1/2 teaspoon salt
1 egg yolk
Zest of 1/2 orange
25 ml or 2 tablespoons cold water

<u>For the filling</u>
1.2 pounds or 20 ounces of fresh spinach
4 tablespoons olive oil
1 onion
1 scallion
2 eggs
1 cup heavy cream
Fresh pepper
Fresh nutmeg
1 cup of grated yellow cheese of your choice. Emmental or gruyère are excellent choices

Before you zest the orange wash it in hot water thoughtfully to make sure there is no wax on the peel. Do not skip the orange zest in the dough. It is a game changer for this dish.

Proceed by making the dough. Place the cold butter and the flour in a food processor and mix. Add sugar, salt, the egg yolk and orange zest (spinach and orange are great friends) and mix again. With the food processor still running add a tablespoon of water. Depending on the humidity, it might need a drop more water before the dough becomes one big ball. As soon as the dough turns into a ball, turn the processor off, wrap the dough in plastic wrap and place in the fridge to cool.

Wash the spinach and drain in a colander really well. If you have a salad spinner use it to dry the spinach. If your spinach leaves are too big, cut roughly with a knife. The tart will be much more pleasant to eat with smaller leaves.

Place a heavy saucepan on medium heat and add olive oil. Dice an onion and one scallion and add to the saucepan along with a pinch of salt. When the onions start to cook and become translucent, add the spinach a little at a time, stirring and turning it around in the saucepan. Turn the heat down to the lowest possible degree and cook until most of the liquid has been absorbed. Remove the saucepan from the heat and transfer the spinach to a platter to cool. If there is still juice in the spinach, squeeze it to get rid of the excess liquid. We do not want any of the spinach juice in our tart. Taste for salt. If it tastes completely saltless add some salt, but remember that you will also add cheese later on, so you don't want the spinach to be salty at this stage.

Meanwhile, turn the oven on to 400°F degrees. Butter a tart pan, and with a rolling pin start to roll out the dough. It is very easy to roll out the dough if placed between two sheets of parchment paper. Transfer the dough in the tart pan, prick with a fork and place in the oven for 10 minutes.

In a bowl mix the two eggs, the cream and the cheese. Add pepper and nutmeg. Add the spinach in the same bowl (be sure that the spinach has cooled down).

After ten minutes of baking take the tart out of the oven, add the spinach mixture and return the pan to the oven for another 40 minutes or until the tart is set and has a beautiful golden color.

Serve with a nice salad and smoked salmon and you have a wonderful meal!

When to make it: for a Saturday brunch with friends, starting the weekend in the most stylish way possible.

Red pepper jelly

Our students LOVE this. After they leave Greece, they often write to tell me that they dream of red pepper jelly. It is the most asked for recipe. I make red pepper jelly with peppers from Florina, a region in northern Greece. Florina peppers are famous for their startling taste and aroma. I think that the closest to the Greek Florina peppers are piquillo peppers. In any case, the peppers you are going to use for this jelly should have thick flesh and pleasant aroma.

2 pounds of peppers
A few spicy peppers like Tabasco peppers
1 onion
A pinch of salt
2 pounds of sugar
7 ounces or 200 ml good red wine vinegar

Wash the peppers, remove the stems and seeds and place them in a strainer to let them drain for five minutes. Place the peppers in the food processor, a few at a time, and pulse for a few seconds. We do not want to puree them, we want to maintain some texture. You can also add a few spicy peppers depending on how spicy you want your jelly to be. Place them in the strainer again to drain some of the juices out for another 5 minutes. Dice an onion and add to a pot along with half of the wine vinegar. Add a pinch of salt. Weigh the peppers, and then add them to the pot along with the same amount of sugar. For example: if you have 800 grams of peppers, add 800 grams of sugar. Cook over very low heat for thirty minutes or until the mixture starts to thicken. Taste. Decide if it would be pleasant to add more vinegar or some Tabasco sauce, or both. Depending on the type of peppers and the time of their harvest, their spiciness will vary, so you have to adjust the taste. Continue cooking for five more minutes and check if your jelly has thickened by pouring a tablespoon of liquid on a cold plate. Run your finger through the middle, and if the liquid remains separated for ten seconds, it is ready (eventually it will run together).

Enjoy it with crackers and cream cheese, or with your chicken nuggets!

When to make it: when you run out of it. You always need to have some in the fridge.

Fried Onions

No matter how many of these onions I make, they're never enough. I've never had leftover fried onions. Period. I usually make them for the program's final banquet which takes place one day before the students leave Greece at the end of every semester.
If you make nothing else from this cookbook, I'd suggest you give this recipe a try.

2 big red onions
1 cup flour
1 teaspoon salt
 Oil for frying

Peel your onions and slice with a mandoline very, very thin (all sliced onions have to have the same thickness). Shoot for around 1/16 of an inch thick. A good tip, so that you don't cry your eyes out when slicing the onions, is to open a door or a window, so that there is a draft of fresh air. It works. After you slice them all, spread them out with your fingers, so that there are no solid slices of onion but small thin rings. Arrange on a tray that you have lined up with paper towels, take the tray to a well-ventilated room and let the onions dry for thirty minutes and up to two hours. Do not leave them in a common area of the house. The smell will be unbearable. Place a frying pan on medium-high heat. Place the onions in a bowl with flour and salt and make sure they are well coated. Shake them, to lose any excess flour, and fry them in batches until deep golden. Once you take them out of the fryer, place on kitchen paper, to get rid of any excess oil. They will not be crispy yet, but they will turn crispy about two minutes after you take them out of the frying pan.

When to make them: when you are going to serve steak or any kind of meat. Or any kind of food actually.

Lentils

Then Jacob gave Esau some bread and some lentil stew. He ate and drank, and then got up and left.
So Esau despised his birthright.   *Genesis 25:34*

For generations, Greeks have been eating lentils weekly. It is considered one of the healthiest and most affordable meals. Recently, chefs have started experimenting with lentils, using them in interesting salads or other creative side dishes. I will give you the classic soup recipe. You can also add rice to the soup. Rice actually helps you digest lentils faster, so it is not a bad idea to add some. You may also add some tomato juice in your lentil soup. When preparing legumes try to add the salt towards the end of the cooking process, or the skin will turn tough.

1/2 pound dry red lentils
Pepper to taste
1/2 teaspoon dry oregano
1/4 cup vinegar
1 clove garlic crushed
1 onion, diced
1 bay leaf
1 teaspoon salt
4 tablespoons long-grain rice (optional)
4 tablespoons olive oil

1/2 cup tomato juice, optional

Wash the lentils, add them to a pot with just enough water to cover them, and bring to a boil. As soon as the water begins to boil, drain it out and start all over again, adding enough water this time to last for about one hour of simmering. While the water is still cold add pepper, oregano, vinegar, the garlic, the onion and one bay leaf. Set the heat on low, so that the lentils are boiling very gently. Check on the water after twenty minutes, to see if there is still enough. At this point, also taste the soup to ensure the taste is good. (Keep in mind that we haven't added salt yet). After forty minutes, check on the water level again and taste the soup. You might need to add more vinegar. If you need to add water, add hot water. The lentils should have started to soften, so if you are going to use rice add it at this stage; if they are still hard, wait for another ten or fifteen minutes to add the rice. At this point add the salt. The time needed for the lentils to soften depends on the type and the size of the lentils, and it is usually between 40-60 minutes. When the lentils are almost ready, add the olive oil. We want the olive oil to only cook for a few minutes, to preserve as many vitamins as possible.

When I make lentils at school, I serve them with a variety of appetizers, as all Greeks do. My favorite dish to pair the soup with is cheese pie and good bread, or with a really good grilled cheese sandwich. Another thing I sometimes make with lentils, if the season is right, is snails with garlic and parsley sauce. There are always some funny videos taken of the most reluctant students as they struggle to try the snails.

When to make this: when you come back from hunting and desperately need something to eat.

Beans

If the beans are big you probably need to soak them overnight. Read the instructions on the package.

1/2 pound white beans
2 tablespoons olive oil
2 onions
2 carrots
1 celery stalk
Pepper
1/2 teaspoon oregano
2 fresh tomatoes
1/2 cup of tomato juice
1/2 cup dry white wine
Salt
<u>Optional</u>
Sausage
Arugula

Start by boiling the beans in a pot. As soon as the water starts to boil, drain it out, add cold water and start boiling the beans all over again. One of the reasons for this is to make sure that impurities are removed. Another reason is to stop the outer skin from cooking so that the temperature rises and cooks the beans from the inside out. With beans, the water should be changed twice, adding cold water every time. Only add enough water to boil them to completion on the third time, after having drained them twice. During this boiling and draining process, start cooking the rest of the ingredients. Dice the onions, the carrots and the celery. Bring a heavy saucepan over high heat and add olive oil, the onions, the carrots and the celery. Let it cook until the vegetables start to change color and thereby release the sugars, which means that taste is building up. Add pepper and oregano. If you want to use sausage, now is the time to add it. Let the sausage cook for a couple of minutes and then add the tomato juice and white wine. Scrape the saucepan to remove all sugars stuck at the bottom. Dice the fresh tomatoes and add them to the saucepan as well. Turn the heat down and let this sauce cook for five more minutes. By now you should be changing the water of the pot with the beans for the third time. As soon as the beans start to boil for the third time (make sure that they are simmering on low heat and not boiling hard), add the vegetable/sausage sauce. Cover loosely with a lid and let them boil very softly until tender. The amount of time needed depends on the size and quality of the beans. It can be anywhere from one hour and a half to two hours and a half. Check every thirty minutes to make sure there is enough liquid in the pot. When the beans are almost ready add the salt and check on the water. Turn the heat off when the beans are completely soft and the soup is creamy. Chop some arugula and serve on top of the beans. Keep the leftovers and eat the next day with some fried eggs and sausage. Some people make beans just so they can eat the leftovers the next morning with eggs.

When to make them: On a Friday night, so that you have the leftovers for Saturday's English breakfast.

Chickpeas

Chickpeas are an amazing legume. They are very tasty and very versatile. The disadvantage is that you need to soak them in water overnight before you cook them (this applies whether you are going to make soup, hummus or falafel). You can also use ready-cooked chickpeas, but with a little planning, you will see that it's enjoyable and rewarding to prepare the dry ones, as the taste is superior. I will give you four recipes, which are four of my favorite dishes in general.

Chickpeas Soup with Lemon

1/2 pound chickpeas
2-3 onions
Juice of one or two lemons
1 tablespoon flour
Salt
3 tablespoons olive oil

Chickpea soup is very easy to make and very nourishing.

Place the chickpeas in a big bowl and cover with water. Leave them to soak overnight. Make sure that you have added enough water, as chickpeas will absorb a lot of it and expand. In the morning, drain the water and rinse them very well to get rid of any starch. Place them in a pot with plenty of water over low heat. We want them to boil very gently. Once the chickpeas start to boil, foam will start forming on top of the soup. Remove it with a slotted spoon. After you remove the foam, cut the onions in small dice and add them to the soup. Check every twenty minutes to make sure there is plenty of water left. If you need to add any, make sure it is hot water. It takes one hour and a half to two hours until the chickpeas are soft but not mushy. When they are soft and before you turn the heat off, add salt (do not add the salt earlier because the skin will get tough) the olive oil and the lemon juice in which you have dissolved one tablespoon of flour. By doing this, you make sure that you will get a creamy soup, not a watery one. If your soup is still very thin, scoop out 1/2 a cup of the chickpeas and purée them in a blender. Return the puréed chickpeas to the soup, boil for five more minutes, and then turn the heat off. This trick will thicken up the soup nicely.

You can do most of the cooking in the morning before you go to work and finish it at night.

When to make it: when you start to feel under the weather and you decide to take a sick day tomorrow. That will give you time to soak the chickpeas overnight.

Chickpeas with Eggplants

This is a dish made in some of the Greek islands.

1/2 pound of chickpeas
3 onions
1/2 cup olive oil
2 eggplants
Fresh ground pepper
Juice of 1 or 2 lemons
1 tomato
Salt

Optional
2 red peppers
1 cup of feta cheese
Parsley

Place the chickpeas in a big bowl and cover with water. Leave them to soak overnight. Make sure that you have added enough water, as chickpeas absorb a lot of it and expand. In the morning, drain the water and rinse them very well, to get rid of any starch. Place the chickpeas in a pot with plenty of water and bring to a very gentle boil. Once the chickpeas start to boil, foam will start forming on top of the soup. Remove it with a slotted spoon. After all the foam is removed, cut the onions in small dice and add them to the soup. Check every twenty minutes to make sure there is plenty of water. If you need to add any, make sure it is hot water.

In the meantime, with a peeler, skin the eggplants and dice them in one-inch squares. Sprinkle with salt. Heat a heavy saucepan and add 1/4 cup of olive oil. Add the diced eggplant to the hot oil, stirring very well in the beginning so that the oil dresses all the eggplant pieces. Cook them, stirring very often, until they get a nice deep brown color. Add lots of fresh pepper. Turn off the heat and then stir in the lemon juice and the tomato, cut in one-inch cubes as well. If you are using peppers, cut them in slices and add them to the mixture at this point. Set the saucepan aside.

When the chickpeas begin to soften (after around one and a half to two hours), but are not ready yet, turn the oven on at 420°F. In a deep baking dish, add the chickpeas, 2 tablespoons olive oil, salt and the eggplant mixture. If you want to add feta cheese, be very careful with salt. Make sure that the dish has about a cup and a half of liquid. We do not want a soupy consistency, but we need to have enough moisture before baking it so that we end up with a creamy dish. The amount of water in the dish is the trickiest part of this recipe. It is easier to add water than to subtract it, so be very careful with how much water you add. Cover the dish with a parchment paper and an aluminum foil on top, close the rim well and bake for twenty minutes. Take off the parchment paper and aluminum foil, add the feta cheese and bake for another fifteen to twenty minutes. Remove from heat and taste for lemon or salt. The aim is to be left with a creamy dish in the end. Add minced parsley and serve.

Chickpeas with Chestnuts

This dish is prepared in a very similar way to the previous one. But unlike the island version, this is a mountain recipe. It is one of those recipes that I hesitated serving to 20-year-olds, but I was very pleasantly surprised to find out that the students really enjoy it.

1/2 pound chickpeas
2 onions
2 tablespoons olive oil
1 tomato
Juice of one lemon
Pepper
1 teaspoon salt
4 or 5 ounces chestnuts, preferably in a vacuum package, peeled and pre-boiled
Parsley

Place the chickpeas in a big bowl and cover with water. Leave them to soak overnight. Make sure that you have added plenty of water, as the chickpeas will absorb a lot of it and expand. In the morning, rinse them with plenty of water, to get rid of any starch. Add them to a pot with plenty of water and boil very gently. Once the chickpeas start to boil, there will be foam forming on top of the soup. Remove with a slotted spoon. After you remove the foam, cut the onions in small dice and add them. Check every twenty minutes to make sure there is plenty of water left. If you need to add any, make sure it is hot water. When the chickpeas are almost tender (after around one and a half to two hours), take them off the stove and place them in a deep baking pan. Turn the oven on at 420°F. Cut a tomato in one inch chunks and add to the pan with the chickpeas, along with 1 teaspoon salt and 2 tablespoons olive oil. Take the peeled, pre-boiled chestnuts, and with your hands break them in half. Ideally, you'll end up with big (which we want for texture) and small pieces (which will infuse the sauce with flavor). Add the chestnuts to the pan. Place a parchment paper on the pan and an aluminum foil on top to seal in the moisture and let cook for about 30 more minutes. If you think that there is too much water in the dish, leave it without a cover. If there is no water, add half a cup. We are aiming for a creamy dish at the end. Another trick -in order to thicken up the soup- is to scoop out half a cup of the chickpeas, purée them in a blender and return to the pan, mix well and bake for five more minutes.

I love this dish. The flavors are earthy, comforting, coupled with a rich, luxurious aftertaste.

When to make it: when you are snowed in or when you wish you were snowed in.

Hummus

Last but not least. What can we say about this popular spread? You can make it with canned, or frozen, or any other pre-cooked chickpeas, but the taste will be so much better if you make it from scratch. I believe you will find a deep sense of satisfaction and accomplishment when you make a dish from scratch. Try it.

1 pound chickpeas
3 onions
1/4 cup lemon juice
1 tablespoon pine nuts (you may omit this if you're allergic to nuts)
1 tablespoon Tahini
1 clove garlic
Salt, pepper
3 tablespoons olive oil
1 ripe avocado
1 boiled medium beet

Place the chickpeas in a big bowl and cover with water. Leave them to soak overnight. Make sure that there is enough water, as the chickpeas will absorb a lot of it. In the morning, drain them, rinse them well, and place them in a pot with plenty of water to boil very gently. Once the chickpeas start to boil, foam will start forming on top of the soup. Remove with a slotted spoon. After you remove the foam, cut the onions in small dice and add them to the pot. Check every twenty minutes to make sure there is still plenty of water. If you need to add any, make sure it is hot water. Add salt one hour after you start cooking the chickpeas. It will take one hour and a half to two hours until the chickpeas are soft but not mushy. Turn the heat off and let them cool down for a while.

In a food processor add the lemon juice, pine nuts and Tahini and start working the mixture until it is smooth. Add the garlic, the olive oil and lastly the chickpeas and beat until very smooth. You might need to add 2-3 tablespoons of the water the chickpeas boiled in so that the mixture is smooth and fluffy. Taste and adjust with salt and pepper. Divide your hummus into three parts: make one with avocado, one with beet and one plain; take out one third of the mixture, place in a nice bowl and cover. In another bowl transfer another third of the hummus and with a fork purée a ripe avocado and mix. Make sure it is a dark green one, that will give you a beautiful green color. In the third portion that is still in the food processor, turn the food processor on and add one medium pre-boiled beet, a little at a time until you achieve the red color that you want.

When to make this: when you are invited to a potluck. Serve with pitas. It will be a hit and the centerpiece of the buffet.

Potatoes

Some very practical advice for potatoes is the serving size. Plan for 8 ounces per person, which is approximately the weight of one big potato or two medium ones.

Mashed potatoes

6 big potatoes
Salt
1.5 cup heavy cream
1 or 2 sticks butter (the amount of butter you add is totally up to you)
Freshly grated nutmeg

When you buy potatoes, ask the vendor for the best variety for mashed potatoes. Russets are usually an excellent choice. Wash the potatoes well and peel them. Don't discard the peels: you will use them later. Place the potatoes in a large pot with cold water, add 2 tablespoons salt and bring to a boil. Let them boil softly over medium heat. This next step might sound weird, but trust me on this. Wash the peels very well and place them in a small pot, add water and a pinch of salt and bring to a boil. As soon as the water boils, drain them, discard the water but keep the peels. Transfer the peels back to the same pot. Make sure that the pot is clean. Pour the heavy cream over the peels and bring to a boil over very low heat. Turn the heat off the pot with the peels after two or three minutes of simmering and set aside while the potatoes continue to boil. Why do we do that? The peels have a lot of flavor. By simmering the cream with the peels, the flavor of the peels is transferred to the cream, thus enhancing the flavor of the mashed potatoes. Check if the potatoes are tender; insert a knife in a potato and lift it up. When the potato slides right off, it is ready. Drain the water completely from the pot with the potatoes. With a potato masher, mash the potatoes. Do not use an electric hand mixer at this point, or your potatoes will turn "elastic" and not fluffy. After you have carefully mashed all the potatoes, cut the cold butter in cubes and gradually incorporate it in the potatoes, mixing constantly with a spatula. When all the butter is incorporated add the cream a little at a time through a strainer and discard the peels. You may stop adding cream once you reach the consistency that you like. (Depending on the freshness of the potatoes, you may decide that one cup of cream is enough, if you like the consistency). Grate nutmeg directly on the potatoes and add 1 or 2 tablespoons of salt. Taste. Add more salt if you need to. Put the lid on and let the flavors infuse in the mashed potatoes. It is very important to let the mashed potatoes rest for at least ten minutes before you serve them.

When to make them. For Sunday lunch with Beef Bourguignon.

Baked Baby Potatoes

These potatoes are probably the most favorite side dish at school!

3 pounds baby potatoes
1/3 cup olive oil
1-2 tablespoons salt, preferably sea salt
2 whole cloves garlic
1 teaspoon oregano
1/2 teaspoon smoked paprika
1/2 teaspoon red pepper flakes
White pepper
1/2 teaspoon Mustard powder
Tabasco to taste

Wash the potatoes and place them in a pot with water and salt. Bring to a soft boil. From the moment the water starts to boil, count five minutes, and then with a slotted spoon take them out of the water and place them into a pan. Turn the oven on, at 420°F degrees. Drizzle olive oil and sprinkle salt on the potatoes abundantly and massage them, while they are still hot, so that the olive oil and salt coat the potatoes (you might need to wear a glove because of the heat). It is very important that the potatoes are coated with olive oil and salt completely. I think this is what my grandma meant when she said that you have to put love in the food you prepare. Add the two whole cloves of garlic. Sprinkle the rest of the spices (or use spices that you like). Bake for around 30 minutes or until they start to brown. Check if they are ready by inserting a knife. They should be very tender. If they are not, turn the temperature down to 400°F and bake for ten more minutes. The problem with these potatoes is that they start disappearing the moment you take them out of the oven and before they reach the table. I always end up with about half of what I started with. So make sure you have enough.

One of our students, Aristides Ortiz who was in Greece in the Spring semester of 2014 wrote the following poem about these potatoes:

Potatoes...

Oh, how I've missed ye.

Thy buttery crunch shall forever linger inside the memory of my buds of taste.

Shall I compare thy smell to a summer's day?

A day of rejoicing when my lips hath finally kissed yon salted skin?

Now my days linger with seeking eyes and watery mouth;

Nay!! Watery eyes and seeking mouth,

until the dreams which I've dreamed with ye potatoes,

hath come true.

Oh, dear, sweet Natasa...

Potato Salad

4 big potatoes
Salt
1 cup frozen peas
1 cup frozen corn
3 tablespoons olive oil
3 tablespoons red wine vinegar
1 onion or 3 scallions
Pickles (about 1/3 cup)
1 tablespoon capers
4 tablespoons mayonnaise

Peel the potatoes and cut them in 1/2 inch squares. Place in cold salted water and bring to a soft boil. Let them cook until they are soft but not mushy. In the meantime place the peas in water and bring to a boil in another pot. When the water starts to boil in the second pot containing the peas, add the corn. Once the water starts to boil again, turn the heat off. Drain the peas and corn and place them in a big bowl to cool. Do the same with the potatoes as soon as they are ready. Add a generous amount of salt, the olive oil and the vinegar. Mix very gently. Mince the onions and do the same for the pickles (I suggest about 1/3 cup, but you can add as many or as few as you like). The onions and pickles are the crunchy elements of the potato salad, so do not mince too fine. With your knife, mince the capers very thin. Add to the potato salad. Taste one more time and adjust. Apart from salt, a bit more vinegar could be nice. Keep in mind that we want to achieve an intense but harmonious balance of flavors in our potato salad. Add 3 tablespoons of mayonnaise and keep one to spread on top. Serve with homemade chicken nuggets.

When to make it: when you need to feed a crowd. This dish goes a long way in feeding a big number of people.

Steamed potatoes (or boiled)

6 big potatoes
Salt or
Seaweed (optional but highly recommended)
1/4 cup olive oil
2 tablespoons vinegar
Pepper
Oregano
1/4 teaspoon dry mustard
1 onion in slices
1 scallion minced
1 tablespoon capers

Wash the potatoes thoroughly and cut them into bite-size pieces (1 x 2 inches). If you have a steamer use it to cook the potatoes. It will take around twenty minutes. If you don't have a steamer, place them in a pot and cover them with salt water. Bring to a boil and let them boil for fifteen minutes, drain most of the water and leave about an inch of water in the pot. Put the lid on the pot and turn the heat off. Let them finish cooking with the steam from the remaining water. It should take approximately another 10 minutes, depending on the size and also the freshness of your potatoes. Check if they are done by inserting a knife. The potatoes should be very tender. Take them out of the pot when ready and place them on a platter. Add olive oil and salt or if you have seaweed add half a teaspoon. Seaweed is quite salty and a very interesting spice to have. You will find it in delicatessen stores. It is very tasty and offers plenty of minerals. Add the rest of the toppings while the potatoes are still hot and serve. This is an excellent side dish for a fish meal, or a good lunch if you are on a diet.

When to make it: make it for dinner when you are on a diet.

Baked potatoes with lemon and orange juice

Greeks eat these potatoes with roasted chicken. We call them lemony potatoes and they are very popular. You can bake these potatoes in the same pan as the chicken. I prefer to use different pans to better control the baking time of each ingredient. If you are not very familiar with your oven, or you are cooking larger quantities, I would suggest doing the same.

6 big potatoes
Salt
1/4 cup olive oil
Juice of 1 lemon
Juice of 2 oranges
Freshly ground pepper
Oregano
Thyme
Red pepper flakes
2 cloves garlic
Butter, optional

Peel the potatoes and cut in pieces that are consistant in size. When you cut the potatoes, it's better to cut them in a way that creates as big a surface as possible. If you cut your potatoes in three triangular pieces by making two diagonal cuts, as shown above, your potatoes will absorb more liquids and become tastier. I have gotten in the habit of cutting all my vegetables this way.

Place the peeled potatoes in a pot with cold water, add salt and bring to a boil. Once the water starts to boil, mark five minutes and then remove the potatoes from the water. Place them in a single layer in a pan. Add one tablespoon of salt and the olive oil. Mix well with your fingers so that the potatoes are coated with olive oil. If the potatoes are too hot for you, use a glove. It is important to add the olive oil and the salt while the potatoes are still hot; they will absorb a lot more flavor. Juice one lemon and two oranges, add 1/2 cup of water to the juices and pour over the potatoes. Add fresh pepper, oregano, thyme, red pepper flakes and two whole cloves of garlic. Mix well. Taste the liquid. It should be intense, rich in lemon and generous in salt, to ensure that the final result is tasty. At this point, my grandma would place a smidgeon of butter on each potato. I don't, but it's up to you. Bake in a 400°F degree oven. (If you are also baking chicken place the chicken in the oven first at 430°F, and 30 minutes later lower the heat to 400°F and add the potatoes). After about twenty minutes take the pan out of the oven and with a spatula turn the potatoes over. Even if not all are turned, make sure all the potatoes have been basted with juice. In another twenty minutes baste the potatoes with the pan juices once again. If you are cooking the chicken in another pan, this is the moment when you should take half a cup of juice from the chicken pan to drizzle it over the potatoes. Be careful not to move the potatoes with the spatula at this stage as they will be very soft, and having not formed a crust yet they may get damaged. In any case, make sure there is still liquid at the bottom of the pan. Add water if you need to and shake the pan so that the juices coat the potatoes. In another twenty to twenty five minutes (a total of 60-65 minutes), your potatoes should be ready with a beautiful golden color, crunchy on the outside and juicy and soft inside.

Tip: The reason we boil the potatoes for five minutes, in the beginning, is to ensure that there will be enough moisture in them, in the end. Once the potatoes are harvested, they start to lose moisture; this is why we often end up with dry potatoes. To ensure that your baked potatoes are crispy on the outside and juicy on the inside, use this foolproof method of boiling them for a few minutes before baking them. It yields great results every single time.

When to make them: when you want your potatoes to be the star of the meal.

MEATS AND POULTRY

When choosing vegetables, we can see how fresh and firm they really are, and most importantly, we can smell them and get a pretty good idea of what their taste is. With meat, it is impossible to know what we are really buying just by looking at it, as the elements that predispose the quality of our end product cannot be easily determined. There is no way of knowing the age of the animal, what it was fed, the amount of its daily exercise, the amount of sunlight, its gender... These elements, and many more, influence the quality of our meat. This is the reason why it is imperative to choose our meat supplier carefully. Visit your local butcher shops and choose a butcher who gave you a good cut once and become friends with him. I know my butcher well, I know his wife's health problems, I know the name of her doctor (I am not kidding) and I am friends with his daughter. At Christmas, I make baklava for him. In the seven years that I have worked as a professional cook, the meat I have bought from my butcher has almost always been of great quality. There have only been two times when the quality was not great, which I communicated to him, to make sure that he knows that my expectations are high. When you go to a meat shop and ask for a piece for meat, your butcher has literally dozens of options to offer you. The piece of meat that your butcher decides to give you can make the difference between an average and an exceptional meal. Get to know him and, most important, make sure he knows you. And he likes you.

Chicken Broth

As you get more serious about food and cooking, it would be a good idea to start learning how to cut a chicken. Whole chickens are cheaper and you can use each part in the best possible way. You can use the bones to make chicken broth. Adding homemade chicken broth instead of water in rice, sauces, or casseroles will improve your dishes immediately. You could also ask your butcher (who is now your friend) for good quality bones. Make sure you don't use the end of the chicken's wings for the broth. Chickens do not perspire, so all of their toxins are deposited at the end of their wings. Cut the tips off and throw them away. Place the bones in plenty of cold water in a big pot and bring to a soft boil. Do not add any salt. As the boiling starts, make sure you remove the foam that forms on top. After you have removed the foam, add an onion, cut in four, a carrot and a celery stalk, each one cut in two pieces. If you have other vegetables, like stems of parsley or stems of mushrooms, add them too. Let the water simmer for a couple of hours. Turn the heat off and let the broth cool. When it cools completely, remove the fat that has formed on the top. Strain all the bones out and divide the liquid in individual containers and freeze. I use one litre yogurt buckets as containers for my chicken broth at work. The size works really well for me. At home, you can use the smaller 200ml containers. You can even use ice cube holders for smaller quantities. If you start making chicken broth, you will never go back to not having chicken broth in your freezer.

Baked chicken (with the lemon potatoes)

One whole chicken or 4 chicken legs with thighs + 4 chicken wings
1 tablespoons salt
Fresh black pepper
1 teaspoon oregano
Juice of 1 or 2 lemons
2 cloves garlic
1 teaspoon mustard powder
1/4 teaspoon paprika

Marinade (optional); 2 cups of water, 2 lemons' juice and zest, 2 tablespoons salt, 2 bay leaves, 1 teaspoon oregano, 2 cloves garlic minced, 1 teaspoon whole peppercorns

You can use one whole chicken or you may use only legs for this dish. Buy two chickens for four people, so you can have four legs. Cut the breasts and save for another day. You can also use the wings. Remember to remove the tips of the wings and throw them away. I like to wash the chicken to remove any impurities and bone fragments. Make sure to disinfect the sink after you have washed the chicken. If you have time, marinate the chicken from two to five hours. The final dish will be juicier. Be sure to cover the chicken completely with the marinade. Before you start cooking, take the chicken out of the marinade and dry with a paper towel. Turn the oven on to 430°F degrees. Place the chicken pieces side by side in the pan and sprinkle with salt, pepper and oregano and massage them to make sure the salt is covering all the meat. If you are using a whole chicken stuff it with one whole orange. It will add a lot of aroma and ensure a juicier final chicken. Juice two lemons and add the juice in the pan along with two whole cloves of garlic, mustard and paprika. Place the chicken in the oven. Twenty minutes later, baste the chicken with the lemon juice and the juices that have come out of the chicken. Ten minutes later turn the heat down to 400°F and taste the juice, add salt and pepper or lemon, if needed. If you are adding potatoes in the same pan add them now. Baste every twenty minutes. Baking should take another 60 minutes, about 1.5 hours in total if you have chicken legs or 30 additional minutes if you have a whole chicken. Take a leg out and cut it from underneath to check if it is done, if you don't have a thermometer. If you do have a thermometer, the internal temperature should be 165°F. If there is a hint of pink near the bone it is not ready; return the pan to the oven and bake for another 10 minutes.

You can serve the chicken with green beans and beetroots. It is very tasty and very photogenic!

When to make it: Sunday dinner for a family gathering

Chicken Nuggets or breaded Pork Fillet Medallions

Chicken breast and Pork Fillet (or Tenderloin) have similar traits and can be mutually substituted in recipes. I love pork fillet because it always turns out tender, it is low in toxin accumulation and has a very low fat percentage. This recipe turns out great whether you use chicken or pork. Either one you choose, make sure that it is cooked thoroughly. You could either bake them or fry them if you prefer after you have breaded them. At school, I bake them after I spray them with some olive oil. When I have guests at home, I usually fry them because the crust is somewhat superior when fried.

2 or 3 chicken breasts or two medium pork tenderloins
2 eggs
1 tablespoon mustard
2 tablespoons soy sauce
1 tablespoon honey
2 cups bread crumbs
1 tablespoons salt
1 teaspoon paprika smoked or hot

Slice the meat in 3/4 of an inch thick nuggets. Beat the eggs with the mustard, the soy sauce and the honey and place the sliced meat in the egg mixture to marinate for at least 30 minutes and up to two hours. Thirty minutes before you serve them, turn the oven on at 430°F and oil a baking pan generously--if you are going to bake the meat. If you are going to fry the meat, turn the heat on at medium high and add vegetable or olive oil in a heavy saucepan about half an inch deep.

Mix the bread crumbs with the salt and the paprika of your likeness. Take the meat out of the egg mixture and bread them carefully, pressing each piece in the bread crumbs to make sure that the crumbs are densely covering the meat. Oil a baking pan generously and arrange the meat in the pan side by side if you are to bake the chicken nuggets or pork medallions. I also spray some olive oil on top, using a clean sprayer like the ones you use to spray your plants, to ensure a nice crust on top. Bake for 15 to 20 minutes until they get a beautiful golden color. You do not need to turn them over, but do cut one, to check for doneness, if you do not have a meat thermometer. If you do have one, the internal temperature for chicken should be 165, and for pork 160 degrees.

If you are frying, arrange them on a tray and fry them for 4 minutes on each side or until they turn golden brown. Do not overcrowd the pan or the temperature of the oil will drop too much resulting in soggy nuggets. Make sure to remove foam and burned bread cramps with a slotted spoon between batches.

Serve with potatoes of your choice and red pepper jelly.

When to make this: when you have leftover waffles from breakfast and you don't know what to eat them with.

Greek Chicken soup Avgolemono (egg and lemon)

Avgolemono (αυγολεμονο) means eggs and lemon in Greek and it is the most common *liaison*-thickening agent in the Greek cuisine. It is used in many dishes and it is simply delicious. This recipe is generally very easy, except for incorporating the egg-lemon in the soup which is a bit technical, but if you understand why we are doing what we are doing, I think you'll have it.
This soup is always the first meal served when a group lands in Greece. After 20-25 hours of transatlantic flight, dehydrated, tired, and dizzy, our students devour it. It is almost like medicine in their stomachs.

For four people
2 chicken legs
2 chicken wings
3 liters water
Salt
Pepper
1.5 cup long-grain rice
1 egg yolk
4 tablespoons lemon juice

Wash the chicken and place in a big pot with 3 liters of cold water and a tablespoon of salt. Bring to a boil and then turn the heat down so that it is boiling gently. With a slotted ladle remove any foam that forms on the surface. After one hour of boiling (start counting when the water starts to boil), remove the chicken pieces and let them cool down. Run the soup through a strainer to remove any loose pieces of bone or impurities. Wash the pot and return the soup to the pot and bring back to a boil. Add the rice, a tablespoon salt and pepper. Let the rice boil for about 10-15 minutes. Make sure that the rice does not get overcooked. In a clean bowl place the egg yolk and three tablespoons of lemon (you might need to add more later). Whisk it up well and while you are whisking vigorously add a ladle of the hot soup. We want to cook the egg yolk first and not throw it in the soup uncooked, because we will end up with an omelet in our soup. Add another ladle of the soup and then the third one, while still stirring the egg mixture zealously. This is the only technical difficulty - adding the hot liquid one spoonful at a time to the egg-lemon mixture while stirring constantly so that the egg does not curdle. (The exact same technique is used in making pastry cream, so now you are ready to make pastry cream from scratch; see creme Anglaise recipe for upside-down apple cake, page 144). Now return the egg-lemon mixture to the soup through a strainer (to catch any egg clumps that cooked too rapidly) and mix well. Take the pot off the heat and add half a cup of cold water to lower the temperature and stop the cooking. Now taste. Does it need a little bit more lemon or salt or pepper? Add carefully. It takes two or three adjustments for any cook to get it to the right point.
Back at the chicken pieces, remove the skin, pick and discard all the bones. Sprinkle salt and pepper on the chicken pieces to enhance the flavor; now you have three choices: 1. Add them to the soup. 2. Make a chicken pot pie. 3. Make a salad; wash and cut some Romaine lettuce and add corn. Sauté the chicken pieces lightly with olive oil, so that they get a nice color and add them to the salad. Dress the salad with a mixture of 4 tablespoons olive oil, one tablespoon balsamic vinegar and one teaspoon mustard after you beat it up to a nice dressing.

When to make it: when it is cold outside and you are feeling under the weather.

Chicken Volcano

This recipe calls for free-range chicken for the simple reason that the flavor of the dish depends solely on the quality of the chicken. The original recipe in my grandma's recipe book from 1950 called for the sauce to be made with milk instead of white wine. I am sure it would still be good, but the wine adds a nice intensity because of the acidity it brings to the sauce.

There is always a lot of excitement at school when I serve this dish.

Half free-range chicken
1.5 cups long-grain rice
Salt
1/2 cup frozen peas
1/2 cup frozen corn
Juice of one lemon
<u>Sauce</u>
2 tablespoons butter
2 tablespoons flour
1/2 cup white wine
Pepper

In a big pot add 3 liters of water and half a chicken: one leg, one breast, one wing. If you cannot cut it or buy it like that, use two thighs with legs rather than breasts because we need a tasty broth and the legs do a better job at that. Bring to a boil over medium heat and add one tablespoon of salt. Skim the foam that forms on the surface. After 60 minutes of simmering, take the chicken out. Let it cool, discard the skin and pick and discard all the bones. Cut the meat in bite size pieces and add salt and pepper. Set aside and keep warm. Read the instructions on your rice package. You will need one and a half cups of uncooked rice and usually, that would take four or five cups of liquid. Remove the amount of liquid you need for your rice out of the broth and pour it through a strainer into a clean pot. Bring to a boil. Add the rice and salt. At this point, the broth should be over-salted. If it is not salty the rice will turn out bland in the end. Five minutes before the rice is ready according to the package instructions add the peas and one minute later add the corn. Let it come to a boil again, add the juice of one lemon and adjust the salt. Turn the heat off and cover with a kitchen towel and a lid and let the steam in the pot finish the cooking of the rice. In the meantime, in another pot, melt two tablespoons of butter. Add two tablespoons of flour and after all the flour is incorporated add 1/2 a cup of white wine and 1.5 cups of the broth through a strainer. Add salt and pepper to taste. Cook while stirring constantly until it thickens up to a silky sauce. If you can still taste the wine or the sauce is too thick add a little more broth. Strain the remaining broth, divide in portions and freeze for future use in sauces or soups.

When all three components are ready, rice, chicken and sauce, start assembling the dish. All ingredients should be warm. Take a Bundt form and fill 1/3 of it with rice. Add a layer of chicken and finish with rice. With a spoon press the rice to sit well in the form. Take a big platter and place it over the Bundt form and turn the whole thing upside down while holding the platter firmly to unmold the rice-chicken dish. Fill the middle hole with sauce and sprinkle with fresh pepper. The name of this dish is actually Chicken Milanese but the students call it "Chicken Volcano." You can see why.

When to make this: when you are wanting to experience a trip to Hawaii without burning a hole through your wallet.

Beef Bourguignon

This is a famous recipe that has been reproduced countless times and even referred to in movies. It is an impressive recipe that has unfailingly resulted in memorable meals; the meat turns out tender and deeply flavored. The reason I decided to include this well known recipe is that I am offering a little trick to make the preparation of this magnificent dish a little less intimidating. I have found that the beef tastes better the next day, so I start cooking it the day before and finish it the day I serve it. By doing that, you don't have to be overwhelmed the day your guests arrive with the undoubtedly complicated preparation but you can focus on something else and enjoy the day. I have also simplified it slightly, just so that the final taste is not compromised. Do not simplify it anymore (I have tried it, believe me) because then the final taste does not have the same intensity and depth.

You could also double the recipe and save a portion in the freezer for later use. I do it all the time and It turns out great. Stop at step 8, if you do that.

6 slices of bacon
3 pounds of beef cut in bite size chunks. Brisket works wonderfully, or any type of stewing cut.

4 tablespoons olive oil
1 tablespoon flour
1 red onion in small dice
1 carrot in small dice
1 celery stalk in small dice
Salt and fresh pepper
Dry mustard
2 tablespoons tomato paste
2 fresh tomatoes
2.5 cups red wine (the recipe calls for bourguignon, but I usually use a medium price range red Bordeaux)

2-3 cups of chicken broth (if you do not have homemade broth, ask your butcher for a bone with marrow and add it to the meal. You have to take it out of course before you serve)

Thyme (fresh or dry) with parsley stems and 2 bay leaves. Tie them together in bouquet garni as seen on page 13. Make two of them, one big one smaller. Use the parsley leaves for decoration at the end.
1 pound of mushrooms, peeled (see Sautéed mushroom recipe page 54) and cut in quarters
3 red onions in slices
1 clove of garlic, smashed

Step 1. Take the meat out of the fridge and place on kitchen paper towels. Dry the pieces and let its temperature rise a little while you do step 2.

Step 2. Cut the bacon in a quarter of inch cubes and add them to a small pot with water. Bring to a boil for two minutes. Turn the heat off and drain the bacon through a strainer. Discard the water but keep the bacon. Do not skip this step.

Step 3. Place a big pot over high heat and add three tablespoons olive oil. Place the beef pieces in the pot so that there is some distancing between them. We don't want to overcrowd the pot, because the meat will not take the beautiful brown color fast enough, and we will lose juices and flavor. Turn the meat around to brown on all sides. Remove and place the browned pieces in a pan. Continue until all the beef is browned. During the browning of the meat, a chemical reaction called the Maillard reaction takes place, which is responsible for the creation of the deep flavors. There are thousands of articles written about that, and chefs are understandably obsessed with it.

Step 4. Turn on the broiler in your oven and wait until it gets hot. Sprinkle the meat with one tablespoon of flour and place the pan in the oven on the lowest rack possible for five minutes. We do not want to cook the meat, we just want to heat up the flour. This is a step that many versions of the recipe skip. Do not skip it. It adds deep flavor to the meat.

Step 5. In the same pan (do not wash it) that you cooked the meat add the onion, the carrot and the celery. You may need to add a little olive oil, if the pan is dry. Add salt to the vegetables, fresh pepper and 1 teaspoon of dry mustard. Let them cook until they start to get a wonderful golden color. Add the bacon and cook for two more minutes. Add the tomato paste and stir.

Step 6. Add the wine and the broth and with a wooden spatula scrape the bottom of the pan well. Puree the two fresh tomatoes and add them too.

Step 7. Transfer the meat back to the pot of vegetables and add the big bouquet garni. Let it come to a boil and then turn the heat down to a gentle simmer amd cover with a lid loosely. The meat should be barely simmering. Taste and add a pinch of salt. Because a lot of the juice will evaporate, do not add all the salt yet. You will adjust the salt at the final step.

Step 8. Let the pot simmer for one and a half hours approximately. During this time make sure there is enough liquid (there should be if the heat is low) and stir every now and then very gently. One way to stir is to shake the pot. After one and a half hours turn the heat off. Cover the meat directly with a piece of parchment paper that you have cut in a circle so that the meat does not discolor (see page 12). Let it cool completely and then put the pot in the fridge for one or even two nights. If you want to serve the meat the same day, you can, just continue the cooking for 30 more minutes. In this case test the tenderness of the meat before you turn the heat off.

Step 9. Next day. Take the pot out of the fridge, bring back to a soft boil. It will need approximately another half hour of cooking to become extremely tender.

Step 10. Meanwhile, peel the mushrooms, slice them and add salt. Place a heavy saucepan over high heat. When it is very hot add 2 tablespoons olive oil and the mushrooms in one layer. Brown them well in batches if you need to. Once all mushrooms are browned, transfer them back to the saucepan. Add the three sliced onions. If the pan is dry add one tablespoon olive oil. Cook for a few minutes and add a crushed clove of garlic. Cook for thirty more seconds and add 1/2 cup of the red wine and the small bouquet garni. When the wine evaporates add one cup of the meat sauce to the mushrooms and cook for ten more minutes on very low heat.

Step 11. Taste. Adjust for salt and check that the meat is very tender. Remove the bone (if you have one) and the two bouquet garnis (from the meat and from the mushrooms). Place the meat on a platter and the mushrooms on top. Sprinkle with minced parsley and serve with mashed potatoes or sautéed vegetables. Or both!

Bon Appetit.

When to make it; when your crush is coming over for dinner.

Ground meat sauce

This is the basic meat sauce recipe. I usually make a big batch and freeze it in portions, to have it ready for pasta Bolognese or whatever I might need to make that calls for it. Lasagna, the Greek Pastichio and Moussaka need this meat sauce.
It's a good recipe to have mastered.

2 pounds of ground beef
3 tablespoons olive oil
1 onion
1 carrot
1 celery
Salt
Fresh pepper
Mustard powder
Thyme
1 cup white or red wine
1 cup tomato juice
1 fresh tomato
1 cup of chicken broth or one bone with marrow

Place a big pot over high heat and add 3 tablespoons olive oil. Add the ground meat and with a wooden spatula or a sturdy whisk start hitting the ground meat. We want to break any lumps in the meat to end up with a fine texture in our sauce as we fry the meat. Keep breaking any lumps and frying the ground meat for a few minutes. After all the meat is browned, add the onion, the carrot and the celery, all cut in small dice along with some salt. If there is no visible fat at the bottom of the pot, add some olive oil. Cook the sauce for five minutes and then add pepper, mustard powder and dry thyme. Cook for another five minutes. It is very important to let the spices heat up with the oil, because they will release wonderful flavors and add a lot of depth to the final dish. In fact, the timing of adding the spices is a very important factor in the final flavor. In general, we add the spices as early as possible and the green, fresh herbs as late as possible. Back to the meat: add the wine, the tomato juice, one fresh tomato pureed and the chicken broth. Scrape the bottom of the pot so that all burned sugars go to the sauce. If you have no chicken broth get a bone with marrow from your butcher and add it. If you add just water, it is not the end of the world. Lower the heat and let the meat sauce simmer for at least thirty minutes or, better, one hour, stirring every now and then. The longer you cook it the deeper the flavors. Italian grandmas cook this meat sauce for four (4!) hours. If you need to, add some water. Taste and adjust the salt.

Place a piece of parchment paper cut in a circle, on top of the meat, so that the meat does not turn dark (page 12) and let the meat sauce cool down completely. Divide into usable portions and freeze any amount you are not using in the next three days.

Pastichio

Maybe the most identifiable Greek dish after the Greek salad is the pastichio. Pastichio is pasta, meat sauce and béchamel sauce, baked in the oven. It is very similar to lasagna in its ingredients but in a slightly different form. You can make two pans of pastichio and freeze one for later use. It freezes very well.

1 pound of pasta, preferably the thick pastichio pasta, but penne will work just as well
1/2 pound of meat sauce, recipe on the previous page (if you make it the day before and use it cold, it's even better)

salt
3 tablespoons butter
4 tablespoons flour
3 cups milk
2 eggs
1 cup grated mozzarella
Pepper
Fresh nutmeg

In a large pot bring about 3 quarts water to a boil. When it starts to boil add two tablespoons of salt and immediately the pasta. Boil for a minute less than the instructions on the pasta packaging. Save one cup of the water the pasta boiled in, drain the pasta and return it to the pot. Add the ground meat sauce to the pasta and mix gently so that the sauce dresses all the pasta. We prefer the meat sauce to be cold (made the day before) because it will cause the temperature of the pasta to drop faster, making it easier for us to handle it. Beat two egg whites slightly and add to the pasta mixture, along with a teaspoon salt. If the pasta is dry add a few tablespoons of the pasta water we saved earlier. If our meat sauce had enough moisture there is no need to do that. Mix well but gently. Arrange in a 9 x 12 inch pan and turn the oven on at 420°F.

Make the béchamel sauce. Melt the butter in a pot over medium heat. Add the flour and cook for one minute stirring constantly. Add the milk gradually while stirring with a whisk until it thickens up to a silky sauce. If the sauce thickens too much, add more milk, if it is too thin continue cooking until you achieve the desired consistency. We want a silky texture that will run between the pasta, as shown in the picture. We do not want it to be too thick because it will stay on top of the pasta like a brick. Take the sauce off the heat. Add salt and pepper and the two egg yolks and mix well. Taste the sauce for salt, it should be very pleasant.

Back to the pasta, sprinkle the mozzarella on top of the pasta and then add the béchamel sauce. Fresh nutmeg adds a delicate, nostalgic aroma and I suggest you try grating a little on top of the béchamel. Bake until wonderfully golden brown.

When to make it: on a Sunday for a family gathering.

Spinach Lasagna DuBois

Lasagna is a wonderful and very versatile dish. You can use any ingredients you like and have a vegetarian lasagna or a meat lover's one. My favorite is a combination of spinach and meat. Our boys devour this dish and I make it multiple times when we have groups with a lot of boys. They have named the dish Lasagna DuBois.

3 tablespoons tomato sauce
One package of lasagna that does not need boiling (you will need about half a pound)
3/4 pound of juicy meat sauce (page 103)
5 tablespoons butter
6 tablespoons flour
3.5 cups milk
Salt
Pepper
Nutmeg
1 cup frozen spinach thawed
1 cup mozzarella
1/2 cup ricotta cheese

Let the spinach thaw. Squeeze the thawed spinach to remove excess moisture.

Make the béchamel sauce. Over medium heat melt the butter and add the flour. When all the flour is incorporated, start adding the milk, one cup at a time mixing very well with a whisk. We want a thick sauce initially, so 3 cups of milk should be enough at this stage. Add one teaspoon salt; it is very easy to end up with salty lasagna because of the cheese you will add later, so be careful with the salt. Once your sauce has thickened up nicely take out half of it and add it to the spinach. If the spinach is not completely thawed, do not worry, it will thaw completely in the hot béchamel sauce. Mix well and set aside. In the remaining béchamel sauce add half a cup more milk and mix over the heat for three or four more minutes. We want a thinner sauce that will cover the top of our lasagna nicely. Set aside.

Preheat the oven at 420°F. If you have homemade tomato sauce you can use it. Otherwise use 4 tablespoons of your favorite tomato sauce on the bottom of a 9 x 12 inch pan. My theory is that the success of the lasagna in part depends on this sauce, as this is the base of the lasagna. Arrange a layer of lasagna on top of the tomato sauce. Check if the spinach has thawed completely in the béchamel sauce and add it on top of the lasagna (warm it up a little if it hasn't). Sprinkle the ricotta cheese on the spinach mixture evenly and smooth the surface of the spinach as much as possible. Add another layer of the lasagna and then add the meat sauce and spread it evenly. Spread half of the mozzarella cheese on the meat sauce. Add another layer of lasagna and end the layering with the rest of the béchamel sauce. Add pepper and preferably fresh nutmeg. Freshly grated nutmeg brings a deep flavor and delicate aroma to the dish. Bake in the oven for 30-40 minutes. When the top of the lasagna starts to take a golden color, take the dish out of the oven, spread the rest of the mozzarella on top, and return to the oven for five more minutes. We do that so that the cheese melts nicely but doesn't burn.

When to make it: when your childhood friends are coming over to watch Sandlot. Make S'mores for dessert.

Soutzoukakia: Greek Meatballs

Soutzoukakia are elongated meatballs with cumin in tomato sauce. If you skip the cumin they are not soutzoukakia. I hate that the plethora of spices needed for the soutzoukakia might intimidate some people from making them, but believe me, the flavors are so deep that you will not regret it. Because of the tasteful red sauce, they are perfect with French fries or mashed potatoes. They are not bad with rice either.

1.5 pound ground beef (you could also use half beef, half pork)
2 tablespoons olive oil
1 tablespoon vinegar
1 onion minced very finely
1 clove of garlic crushed
1 teaspoon dried oregano
1/4 teaspoon cumin
1/4 teaspoon turmeric
1/4 teaspoon hot paprika
1/4 teaspoon dry mustard
1/4 teaspoon pepper
4 slices of good bread (preferably not the white store-bought kind)
1 tablespoon salt

Sauce
4 tablespoons olive oil
1 onion
Salt
Pepper
1/2 teaspoon cumin
2 fresh tomatoes
1 jar of tomato juice
1/2 cup of wine (preferably red, but white works as well)

Place the bread in a bowl with water to soak. Mix the ground meat with the olive oil, the vinegar, and the rest of the ingredients, except the bread and the salt. Mix well for three or four minutes. Take the bread out of the water and squeeze slightly some of the water out, but not completely, and add it to the meat along with the salt and mix well. At this point, you have to try the meat. If you feel uncomfortable, just try a little and spit it out. Believe me, it will not harm you. (French people eat raw ground meat all the time). You should be able to taste both the salt and the cumin. If not, add some more. We want to have soft and juicy ground meat, a lot looser than when we started, but not too loose or our meatballs will fall apart when cooked. The consistency should resemble that of a soft dough. If you think you went too far, and your meat is too loose, add one egg to hold it together. Form the meatballs and cover them with plastic wrap. Place in the fridge for the spices to infuse while you are making the sauce.

Cut the onions and the tomatoes in big dice; we will puree them later. (If you do not have a hand blender to puree them, cut them very fine now). Bring a heavy saucepan over high heat and add olive oil, the onion and some salt. Let the onion cook until it starts to get a nice golden color. Add the pepper and the cumin to the onion and let them cook for one minute until their aromas are released in the oil. Add the fresh tomatoes cut in cubes, the tomato juice and the wine. Add a cup of water, let it come to a boil and turn the heat down. Let the sauce simmer for at least fifteen minutes. The longer you cook the sauce the deeper the flavors but make sure there is enough water. Taste and adjust the salt. Take the pot off the heat and with a hand blender puree the sauce until the texture is smooth. Bring back to the heat on low and very carefully add the meatballs. Cook for another twenty minutes and your soutzoukakia are ready!

When to make them: when you want to treat yourself.

Pork fillet with raisins

2 medium size pork fillets
Olive oil
2 tablespoons butter
Salt, pepper
1 onion minced
1/2 teaspoon dry mustard
1/2 teaspoon dry thyme
4 tablespoons cognac
1/2 cup sweet red wine, Mavrodafni (Greek wine) or Porto (Portuguese wine)
1 tablespoon balsamic vinegar
1 cup chicken broth
1/4 cup golden raisins
2 tablespoons pistachios
1 tablespoon butter

Preheat the oven at 420. With a paper towel pat the pork fillet dry. Place a heavy saucepan over high heat. Add 2 tablespoons olive oil and 2 tablespoons of butter. As soon as the butter melts, place the fillets in the hot saucepan and start browning them. Sprinkle them with half a teaspoon salt and a pinch of pepper. When you have achieved a nice deep brown all around take them off the heat and transfer them to a pan. Sprinkle the filets with fresh pepper again, a pinch of thyme and a pinch of dry mustard. Place in the oven at 420°F for twenty minutes. If you have a thermometer, the internal temperature should be 160°F. Otherwise, check by inserting a fork. The juices should be clear. Take the meat out of the oven, cover it with aluminum foil and let it rest for at least ten minutes.

Meanwhile, back to the saucepan: add the minced onion (you might need to add a tablespoon of olive oil too) and cook until it starts to get a golden color. Add dry mustard and thyme and stir for one minute. Add the cognac and thirty seconds later add the sweet red wine, the chicken broth and the balsamic vinegar. Make sure you scrape the bottom of the pan. Turn the heat down and cook until the volume of the sauce is half of what you started with fifteen minutes earlier. Taste the sauce. We are looking for a good balance of sweet from the wine, salty from the meat and sour from the vinegar. Adjust the taste by adding either more vinegar or a teaspoon of honey if it needs more sweetness, and turn the heat off. We want to remove the onion, so transfer the sauce through a sieve to another pot.

When you are ready to serve, slice the meat and keep it warm. Back to the sauce: turn the heat on and add the raisins and the pistachios. When it starts to boil again, add a tablespoon of butter stirring constantly, let it cook for thirty seconds and turn the heat off. Serve immediately with white rice or baked potatoes or, even better, sweet potatoes.

Note: you could use the same recipe with chicken breast instead of pork fillet.

When to make it: when you got a raise and you want to celebrate. This is a fancy meal.

Chicken breast *or* pork fillet with lemon

These two types of meat are very similar and can be cooked in similar ways. This recipe suits both very well. It is also the fastest way to cook meat. And it is very tasty, too.

2 tablespoons olive oil
2 chicken breasts
Salt, pepper
Dry tarragon or smoked paprika
2 tablespoons freshly squeezed lemon juice
1 tablespoon butter (optional)
OR
2 tablespoons olive oil
2 pork fillets
Salt
Pepper
Thyme
3 tablespoons freshly squeezed lemon juice
Butter

Slice the chicken breasts in half horizontally so that the chicken is half as thick or cut the pork fillet in 1/2 inch medallions.

If you have a saucepan that is not non-stick, use that. We want the meat to stick and create sugars at the bottom of the pan.

Turn the heat on and when the heavy saucepan heats up well add the olive oil. Add the meat. Sprinkle with salt and pepper and your choice of seasoning. Smoked paprika or tarragon if you are making chicken, thyme if you are making pork. Let it cook until it gets a nice deep brown color, about 4 minutes. Turn on the other side and lower the heat to medium. Cook longer on this side, but wait until the color is just as deep. If you have a meat thermometer check it. For chicken, the internal temperature should be 165°F and for pork 160°F. Otherwise make a small incision in the meat with a sharp knife (you shouldn't really, but there is no other way) and check if it is cooked thoroughly. Both types of meat need to be very well done. If the meat has gotten a really nice color but it is not ready inside, turn the heat to the lowest and turn the meat on the other side a couple of times until it is done. When ready, transfer the meat to a platter and add the lemon juice with two tablespoons of water to the pan. With a wooden spatula scrape the bottom of the pan to deglaze. The juice will start to evaporate fast, but before it does, add a tablespoon of butter, let it melt, and then pour the lemon sauce over the meat. Easy, fast and delicious.

Note. The French use wine to deglaze the pan. Greeks use lemon juice. It does the exact same job since they are both acidic.

When to make it: when you want to impress someone with your amazing and quick cooking skills.

Pilaf

A pilaf is a great addition to your meal. It is very versatile and you can add as many or as few ingredients as you like, apart from the basic ones. We usually call rice a pilaf if it has first been cooked in some kind of fat before the liquid (water or broth) is added.

Use one cup and a half of rice for every 4 people.

5 tablespoons olive oil
1 red onion
1 tablespoon salt
1.5 cup long-grain rice; parboiled or basmati works well. If you use basmati, rinse it first.
2 cups chicken broth (it will not be the end of the world if you just add water)

<u>Optional</u>
2 tablespoons pine nuts
2 tablespoons pistachios
1/2 cup chestnuts (pre-boiled)
1/2 cup raisins
1/2 cup orange juice

Place a deep pot over high heat (if you don't have one, use a regular pot). Add 5 tablespoons of olive oil (I know it's a lot), the onion minced very finely and the salt and cook until the onion becomes translucent. Add the rice and stir with a wooden spoon. Make sure all the rice grains are coated with olive oil. The onion has released its sugars in the oil and now we are letting the rice absorb them. Cook, stirring constantly until some grains begin to brown. Add one cup of chicken broth or, if your meat has white sauce, take a cup of the meat sauce and add it, or just add water. The total amount of liquid you add should be the right one according to the instructions on your rice package (do not forget that you will add 1/2 cup orange juice in the end). Taste for salt. The rice should be quite salty. If it is not salty at this point, it will be tasteless at the end. Check the instructions on the rice packaging and five minutes before the completion of the cooking add these ingredients: nuts, chestnuts cut in half, raisins and the freshly squeezed orange juice. Let it come to a boil again and when it does, turn the heat off, cover with a kitchen towel and the lid and let the rice finish cooking in the steam. The orange juice might surprise you, but it adds a wonderful sweet and sour hint. I absolutely love it. This is our Christmas rice and we serve it with turkey.

When to make it: at Christmas! And every winter Sunday after that.

Linguine with garlic

This has to be my favorite dish to eat and make. Easy, fast and absolutely delicious. Unbelievably delicious.

1 pound linguine pasta
2 tablespoons salt
4 tablespoons olive oil
3 cloves garlic
Sea salt or seaweed salt
Pepper
A handful of cherry tomatoes
Red pepper flakes
Parmesan or your choice of cheese

In a big pot add 3 quarts of water and bring to a boil. Add 2 tablespoons salt and the pasta. Stir every three or four minutes while the pasta is boiling. Meanwhile, in a small pot over the lowest heat possible add the olive oil and the three cloves of garlic, sliced as thinly and as evenly as possible. Do not leave it unattended as long as the heat is on and the garlic is infusing the olive oil because the garlic can burn very fast. It will take around 5-7 minutes for the garlic to take a nice golden color. Turn the heat off immediately and leave it on the stove. Back to the pasta: before you drain it, save a cup of the water the pasta is boiling in. You might need to warm up the leftover pasta later, or you might decide to mix some cream with parmesan; the starchy water will help you make a thick delicious sauce. Always save a cup of that water. (And if you finally end up not using it, water your plants with it. They will be grateful). Take the pasta off the heat one minute before the instruction on your pasta box and drain it. Do not rinse the pasta. Never rinse the pasta except maybe (depending on the recipe) when you are making pasta salad. Return the pasta to the pot and add the olive oil and garlic to the pasta. Add a couple of tablespoons of pasta water to bring in some moisture. Add a handful of cherry tomatoes cut in half, a good pinch of sea salt, fresh pepper, red pepper flakes, and grate some parmesan. Serve immediately.

This is the perfection of simplicity.

Note: No matter what kind of sauce I am making, I almost always add this garlic olive oil. It makes the pasta tastier. Our students love it.

According to my camera, the time lapse between these two images is fourteen minutes. Only.

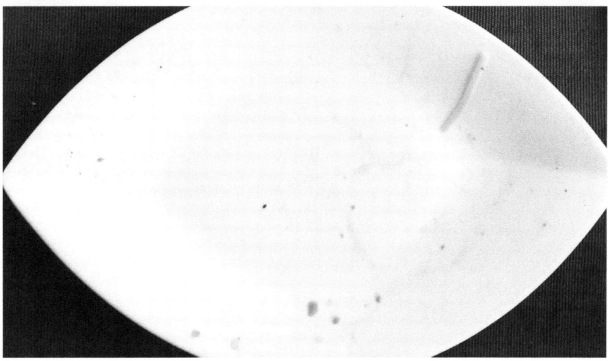

Pasta with Salmon casserole

This version of Pasta with Salmon was created completely by chance. I had served Vitello Tonnato (an Italian dish) for lunch. There was some leftover sauce that I decided to use that night for the dinner meal. The Italian dish is made with a beef based sauce with mayonnaise and anchovies. The marriage of this sauce with the Salmon casserole was unbelievably tasty.

Olive oil
1 pound salmon
1/4 cup Vodka

Olive oil
1 onion
1 scallion
Salt
1/2 pound of spinach or 1/4 pound asparagus (if it is spring)
1 pound of rigatoni or penne

Sauce
1 cup chicken broth
2 tablespoons Worcestershire sauce
3-4 anchovies
4 tablespoons mayonnaise
2 tablespoons butter
2 tablespoons flour

Alternatively, you may skip this sauce completely (last six ingredients) and make a simple one with 2 tablespoons butter, 2 tablespoons flour, 2 cups chicken broth + 1/2 cup white wine (see page 98, the sauce recipe for the Chicken Volcano).

With a good knife skin the salmon. Take out any bones and cut them into 3/4 of inch cubes. Add salt and pepper. In a heavy saucepan heat up olive oil and add the salmon, cook for two minutes and turn the cubes around for one more minute. Add the Vodka. If you are confident and your kitchen has space, light it up to burn the alcohol fast. If there is any chance that you will burn your house down, skip this step. The alcohol will burn out in two minutes. Turn the heat off, transfer the salmon to another bowl and set aside. If you feel that the salmon is not cooked thoroughly, remember that we are putting the dish in the oven later.

In a big pot bring 3 quarts of water to a boil and add 2 tablespoons salt and the pasta. Cook until al dente, two minutes less than the instructions. Save a cup of the boiling water from the pasta, drain the pasta and set aside.

Preheat the oven to 420°F. In the same saucepan, you cooked the salmon add one tablespoon olive oil and one onion and scallion, minced. Add a pinch of salt and cook for a few minutes. Add the spinach and stir it around until it loses its volume. If you are using asparagus and not spinach, snap off the bottom one inch or one inch and a half and discard. Cut the asparagus into two-inches long pieces and cook them (without the onions) in 1/2 cup of water. When all the water has evaporated add one tablespoon olive oil and a pinch of salt and cook them for two more minutes until they get a nice golden color. Transfer to another bowl and set aside. Set aside.

In a food processor add the anchovies with the mayonnaise and the Worcestershire sauce and blend until smooth. You should not be intimidated by the anchovies, you won't be able to taste them in the end, they just add a lot of flavor. In the same saucepan you used before, melt two tablespoons of butter, add the flour and when all the flour is incorporated add a cup of broth and a cup of water. Stir well for a couple of minutes and then add the mayonnaise mixture and cook on very low heat for two more minutes. You should have a slightly thick sauce that will dress all the pasta nicely. If you feel that the sauce is too thick and will not spread to the whole pasta add half a cup of pasta water.

Mix all the ingredients, the salmon, the pasta and the spinach or asparagus and arrange in a casserole dish. Pour the sauce over them. If you don't want to make this sauce make a simpler version. Melt 2 tablespoons butter, add the flour and then add 2 cups chicken broth and half a cup white wine. Cook for four or five minutes until it thickens up slightly.

The pasta will fit nicely in a 9 X 12 pan. Bake for 15 minutes at 420°F. Remember that all the ingredients are cooked but we just want to create a nice crust on the top.

When to make it: when you just found out that you need to watch your cholesterol.

Pasta with shrimp

This is probably the most typical gourmet Greek dish. Almost all of the fancy restaurants in Greece serve a version of this dish. Try to make it with whole shrimp in the shell; the taste will be phenomenal. Most of the taste of the shrimp is in the head. I will walk you through how to clean the shrimp and make this unbelievably tasty sauce. If you buy the shrimp frozen, open the packaging and let them thaw in the fridge, covered with a wet towel. If you buy them fresh, keep them also in the fridge with a wet towel covering them, until you are ready to use them.

Calculate 3 to 5 shrimps per person depending on their size, so between 20-30 shrimps for six people. The cleaning of the shrimp is time consuming, so keep that in mind.

20-30 shrimps in the shell
3 tablespoons olive oil
1 onion finely chopped
2 cloves garlic, crushed
1/4 cup Greek ouzo (alternatively you could use Vodka or white wine)
3 fresh tomatoes in small dice
Tomato juice in a box
2 pounds linguine pasta or your choice
Parsley
1 tablespoon sugar (optional)

Have three bowls ready before you. Cut off the heads of the shrimp. You will collect the heads in one bowl, the flesh in another and the shells in a third one. Run your thumb along the legs to break the shell. Once the shell has broken, it should peel off when you glide your thumb one more time along the leg line. With two fingers squish the tail and pull it out. Now we need to devein the shrimp, which means taking out the intestine on the back of the shrimp. Place a toothpick perpendicular to the body of the shrimp on the top, underneath the black line where the two shells meet, and simply pull up. The black intestine line should come out. Discard just that. A kitchen paper towel will help you collect all the intestine and clean the toothpick. Take the clean shrimps and keep them in the fridge wrapped with a wet towel until the time comes to use them. In a small pot boil the shells in two cups of water for 15 minutes. Some people boil the pasta in that water, but I prefer to use it in the sauce.

And now, let's start with the delicious sauce. In a heavy saucepan, over medium heat, add 2 tablespoons olive oil and the heads of the shrimps. With a potato masher, start squeezing the heads. Remember that you are trying to squeeze out all the tasty juice off the heads. After you do that for about five minutes, add the onion, fresh pepper and a pinch of salt. Continue squeezing. When the onions begin to soften, add one clove of garlic crushed, and 30 seconds later add the Ouzo or Vodka or wine. Ouzo has a licorice aroma which is amazing with fish and seafood. Let the alcohol cook for a couple of minutes and then add the fresh tomatoes (pureed) and the tomato juice. Now add the water that you boiled the shells in. Discard the shells. Taste for salt and add a lot of pepper. Turn the heat down and let it cook for 15-20 minutes. Taste the sauce and if it is too acidic add a tablespoon of sugar. Remember that the heads have all the taste. I like to serve them on the pasta so that the more adventurous guests can nibble on them. They are extremely tasty.

When you are almost ready to serve, bring about 3 quarts of water to a boil in a big pot. When it starts to boil, add a tablespoon of salt and the pasta. Stir the pasta every 3-4 minutes. In a saucepan over high heat add one tablespoon of olive oil and one minute later the shrimps. Cook for two minutes, turn the shrimps over and add a clove of crushed garlic. Cook on the other side for one more minute and then add the sauce. We do not want to cook the shrimps too much, as they become chewy when they are overcooked, so we take the sauce with the shrimps off the heat two minutes later.

Save a cup of the pasta water. Drain the pasta two minutes before the instructions suggest and immediately return it to the pot along with the shrimp sauce. If you feel the sauce is too thick, add the pasta water and stir very carefully. Leave the pasta in the sauce over the hot stove for one more minute to let the pasta absorb all the goodness. Serve immediately with pepper and parsley.

If serving the heads of the shrimp is too weird for you, you may remove the heads from the sauce. Do exactly what we described earlier, just cook the sauce for 10 minutes longer to ensure that you have taken as much taste off the heads as possible. Pass the sauce through a sieve, squeezing really well, so that all the taste from the heads is transferred to the sauce. Fry the shrimps with the garlic as described earlier and add them to the pasta along with the sauce.

Cleaning of the shrimp requires some time, but it is so worth every minute.

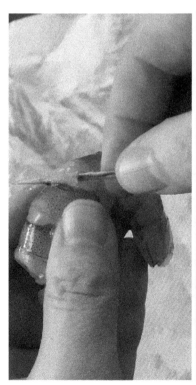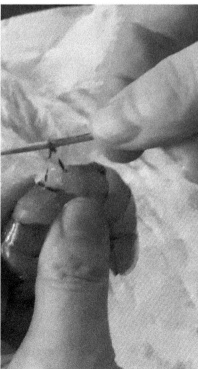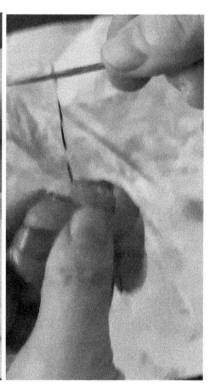

When to NOT make it: when you just found out that you need to watch your cholesterol.

Five-minutes Snacks

We all get hungry at some point and crave something delicious, easy and interesting to eat between meals. Here are a few ideas.

Apple with cinnamon and nuts with Tahini/honey sauce. Tahini is sesame seed paste. Mix two parts of Tahini with one part of honey, stir it up for thirty seconds and it will thicken up slightly, add some cinnamon and you have one of the healthiest snacks you can put in your mouth. Alternatively, you can eat Tahini and honey with bread, just as you would peanut butter. Another choice is Tahini and honey with a piece of good gruyere cheese. It is a fascinating combination with an intense contrast of flavors. Packed with vitamins, minerals and antioxidants, Tahini and honey sauce is a favorite at school. One time Jenna, a dear girl, messaged me two years after she had left Greece to ask the name of the Tahini because she wanted to order it online. When it arrived she messaged me, "Natasa, I am home!"

For me, Tahini and honey on whole grain bread is the ideal breakfast in that I feel full for many hours and have no cravings for sugar for the rest of the day.

Cinnamon is a strong anti-inflammatory and is loaded with antioxidants. Use Ceylon cinnamon. It is a lot healthier than the cheaper one you get at the supermarket and has a much deeper and more complex/sophisticated taste. The good cinnamon (Ceylon) is lighter in color than the cheaper, more common one. The cheap cinnamon has a higher percentage of coumarin, which in very big doses could be harmful.

Cherry tomatoes with olive oil, balsamic vinegar, sea salt and goat cheese. Sprinkle with basil or any herbs you like. This is a refined version of the most common snack in Greece, which is bread with tomato, feta cheese and olives.

Get some really good olive oil and keep some good bread at hand. If you are not using bread very often, keep some in the freezer, sliced. Or alternatively, keep some good quality pitas in the fridge. Warm up the bread or pita and dip it into olive oil that has oregano, thyme, basil, sumac or a combination of them. Add some sea salt and you have a delicious and healthy snack.

Make some porridge with one cup of milk or almond milk (works just as well) and four tablespoons of oat flakes. Cook over low heat stirring constantly until it thickens up, 4-5 minutes. Turn off the heat. Add one tablespoon honey, mix and serve in a bowl. Use any topping you like, red fruit, apple, banana, nuts or even dark chocolate chips. Don't forget to add Ceylon cinnamon for taste and for the nutritional benefits.

Greek yogurt, strawberries or pineapple, nuts and a tablespoon of citrus jam. Here, I am using homemade lemon jam with lemons from our trees. Always keep a couple of good jams in your fridge. Greek yogurt with fruit and nuts is a very common snack in Greece and one with many health benefits. I urge you to research the benefits of yogurt on your health.

Ntakos: this is a Cretan snack. If I were to describe the Mediterranean diet in one picture, this would be it. Get some barley toasts or any other type of double baked bread. Rub them slightly with a garlic clove. Sprinkle them with olive oil, add tomato cut in cubes, sea salt and oregano. Eat with your choice of cheese. Feta cheese is great, or use a softer goat cheese.

Bread with honey and your choice of nuts. Instead of your normal peanut butter and jelly sandwich, spread some good honey on your bread and add chopped nuts. It's healthier and a lot more interesting.

Bread with cream cheese and red pepper jelly (our students go crazy over that). You can use bread or even crackers. I serve this as an appetizer when I have big groups of people over, but it works well as a snack, any time of day.

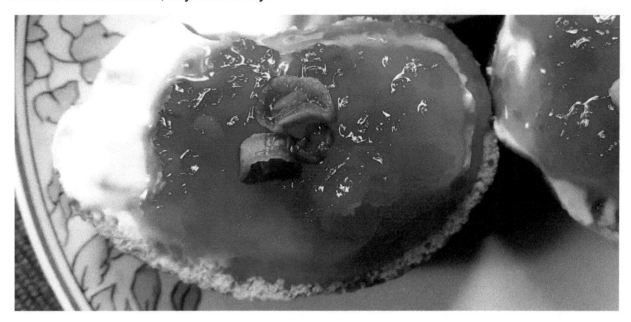

Mix arugula with some parmesan, a drop of olive oil and balsamic vinegar. Place a handful of the arugula on a slice of smoked turkey or the ham of your choice and roll. This is a fancy snack. Eat with bread or crackers and maybe a boiled egg. It is also an excellent keto diet snack.

Cut a green pepper in slices and add to a hot saucepan along with one tablespoon olive oil and a pinch of salt. Cook for two or three minutes. Add a few cherry tomatoes cut in slices and two tablespoons of tomato sauce. Add red pepper flakes and cook for another two minutes, add feta cheese (or a cheese of your choice) and serve on bread.

Last but not least. Get some good Italian prosciutto and pears, strawberries, melon, pineapple or avocado and have one of the tastier and more sophisticated snacks you can have. If you have company, make a platter with various cheeses, fruit and crackers. Enjoy!

DESSERTS

Fruit glacé or candied Orange peels

I debated long and hard if I was going to include this recipe because of the time it takes to complete it. It takes six days! However, the time you actually have to commit to it is very little. It is also a relatively easy recipe once you understand the process of it. *Fruit glacé* is a French technique to preserve fruit but, because it is so time consuming, it is extremely expensive to buy glazed fruit (as I discovered many years ago when I naively chose to buy a box in a beautiful pastry shop in Switzerland!). Enough said.

Six oranges. Preferably get winter oranges that have thick peel
2 pounds of sugar
Pinch of salt
Vanilla extract

Optional
200 grams dark, unsweetened chocolate
Pinch of salt

We do not use the top and bottom discs of the orange peels, we use the peels around the orange as shown in the picture.

Day one. Start by washing the oranges in warm water to remove any protective wax on the peels. Cut and discard the top and bottom of the orange. Score the peel in four or five places from top to bottom so that the pieces can be removed easily. Once you remove all the peel, cut it in 1/4 of an inch wide sticks. Save the oranges in the fridge to eat later. Place all the peels in a deep bowl filled with cold water. Massage them for ten seconds. We want to lose some of the bitter oils of the peels. Before you go to bed, drain the peels and add fresh water, covering them completely.

Day two. Drain them again in the morning and add fresh water. Repeat in the evening.

Day three. Repeat the process. (I told you it wasn't difficult). Before you go to bed place the peels with plenty of water in a pot and bring to a boil. Let them boil for five minutes. Turn the heat off and leave the pot with the water and peels to cool completely, overnight.

Day four. Drain the peels and weigh them. Add the same amount of sugar. For example, if the peels are 500 grams, add 500 grams of sugar. Add enough water to barely cover the peels. Bring to a very gentle boil. Let the peels boil for about 25-30 minutes until they start to become translucent. Stir with a wooden spatula very gently once or twice. You can also shake the pot often to prevent the sugar from burning. Turn the heat off and let the peels cool for at least 12 hours in the pot.

Day five. Turn the heat on again. Boil for three minutes. Turn the heat off and let them cool slightly. Once they are cool enough to handle, take them out of the pot and let them drain in a colander. Arrange on a cookie sheet so that the peels are not touching or if you have one of those pastry racks pictured below, use it. Let the peels dry for 24- 36 hours. They should be dry enough that when you touch them, there is no syrup left on your fingers.

Day six. They are now ready! Place them in an airtight container so that they do not dry further. You could also dip them in chocolate. Melt 200 grams or 7 ounces of chocolate in a *bain marie* (page 12) or in the microwave. When the chocolate has melted add a pinch of salt and mix. Start dipping the orange peels in the chocolate, one at a time, and arranging them on parchment paper to dry. Bon appetit!

When to make them: when you get a promotion make them for your boss. It is a fine gift! Start making them when you first suspect that your boss likes you. They will be ready by the time you actually do get the promotion.

Natasa's lemon yogurt

This is my signature dessert. It is very light and very refreshing and can accompany any meal, any time of day. Extremely easy, extremely tasty and extremely popular.

2 pounds of Greek yogurt, 2% or 5% or even better, whole fat yogurt. Do NOT get 0%.
1 can of sweetened condensed milk.
1-2 lemons, zest and juice (if your lemons are small, you might even need three or four)

Wash the lemons very well in hot water to remove any wax that is coating the peel. Zest two lemons and juice them.
In a nice bowl add the yogurt and condensed milk and mix. Add the zest and the lemon juice a little at a time. You might need the juice of just one lemon, or you might need three. You never know how juicy a lemon is, and you never know how sour the juice is. Taste it, it has to be wonderfully lemony to balance the sweetness of the milk. Cover the bowl with plastic wrap and leave it in the fridge for at least 30 minutes. The lemon thickens the yogurt and we end up with the consistency of a mousse.
Serve with the toppings of your choice. My favorites are strawberries, pineapple or chocolate chips. And, of course, do not forget to add nuts for crunchiness.
I do not think that there is anyone of the 500 plus students who have stayed in Greece for a semester that has not fallen for the lemon yogurt.

When to make it: literally all the time. Stop just before you get sick of it.

Baklava

Baklava is one of the most common desserts in Greece and in many Middle Eastern cultures. There are countless ways, recipes and combinations for making baklava, and my way is not the most typical because I do not like too much syrup, which is not typical. I prefer my baklava crunchy. I also like a subtle orange flavor, so I add orange juice and zest in the syrup. You can pick and choose how you like it. But no matter what recipe you choose to make, there are some rules. Your phyllo dough has to be thin. Because the phyllo dough has no fat, it will dry very, very fast. So get everything ready and then open the package. After you open the package, cover it with a damp kitchen towel. Do not be afraid to improvise with the filling. As long as there is phyllo dough, nuts and sugar, you can call it baklava.

1 package of phyllo dough. Let it thaw in the fridge for at least two hours (and up to three or four days) and then let it come to room temperature on the counter.
1/2 cup olive oil or unsalted butter

<u>Filling A</u>
1/2 pound walnuts
1/2 cup sugar
1 teaspoon cinnamon
A pinch of clove
A pinch of fresh nutmeg
A pinch of salt (or two)

<u>Filling B</u>
1/2 pounds pistachio
1/2 cup sugar
Vanilla
A pinch of salt (again, maybe two)
Zest of one orange (optional)

<u>Syrup for two fillings</u>
2 cups of water
2 cups of sugar
Zest and juice of half an orange

In a heavy saucepan prepare the syrup. Mix the water, sugar and orange zest and juice and bring to a boil for five minutes. Remove from heat and let cool.

You can use olive oil or butter. I actually use them alternatively. If you use butter, melt it over medium heat and let it burn slightly to achieve a deep and wonderful aroma (see page 13). Do not leave it unattended because it goes very fast from a light burn with a wonderful aroma to unusable. Let it cool slightly. Prepare the filling. In a food processor add the ingredients of one filling (do not forget the salt, it brings out all the flavors) and turn the processor on for a few seconds at a time. We want to break the nuts but not end up with a sand-like texture, because chunks of the nuts will give us texture and body and create air pockets, thus fluffiness. Proceed with the second filling if you are doing two. Preheat the oven at 420°F.

Now you have all the ingredients ready. Open the phyllo packaging. Very carefully spread the phyllo flat in front of you, so that the long side is close to you. Butter the phyllo (butter also the pan you are going to use) very generously with the help of a brush. We need a good amount of butter -- two tablespoons per phyllo sheet. Spread three tablespoons of the filling on 3/4 of the phyllo, leaving the farthest 1/4 of the phyllo without filling and start rolling the phyllo as tight as you can. Sometimes the phyllo is very thin and one sheet does not hold, so if your phyllo gets cracks, use two sheets of it at the same time with one filling. Once you have rolled the first baklava cylinder, transfer it to your baking pan. If you use a round pan, place it in a round swirling motion. If you use a rectangular one, place the baklava parallel, one roll next to the other (as seen in the picture). Proceed to the next phyllo, buttering it well and adding the filling. When you are done with all the filling, take a sharp knife and cut the uncooked baklava in the desirable pieces. Butter the top well and with your fingers sprinkle a little water on top of the baklava. A little moisture will make the top phyllo crunchier. Bake for 10 or 15 minutes. By then the baklava should have a nice golden color. Take it out of the oven and very carefully add the syrup on top with a ladle, drenching every piece of the baklava with syrup. Return the pan to the oven. Five minutes later open the oven door slightly to let humidity escape, facilitating the caramelization of the phyllo. Bake for another five minutes and you should have a golden, crunchy, flavorful baklava.

Surprisingly, baklava is the one dessert that gets better with time. Don't get me wrong, it's amazing right out of the oven; it just gets better with time; the flavors get deeper and the phyllo gets crunchier. Save some and eat it twenty days later.

When to make it: any and every time you think of it. It's a great way to impress someone you're interested in with your baking skills and to have a great dessert afterward.

Custard Pie

I made this pie when I first started working at the school and I told the students that it was a Milk pie because that is what we call it in Greek. It was not received with enthusiasm. I was devastated! At my kids' suggestion, I made it again a couple of weeks later but called it Custard pie. It was devoured in five minutes. Anyway, -so- "Custard" pie is a hybrid between smooth cream and crunchy baklava. It has the best elements of both worlds. And it's my husband's favorite dessert.

1/2 package phyllo dough
1 quart or 4 cups milk 3.5 % fat or more (please do not make this with skim milk or 2 %)
1/2 cup fine semolina or regular Cream of Wheat, not instant (you will find it at the flour section)
1/2 cup sugar
Vanilla
A pinch of salt
2 eggs
Zest of one lemon
1 stick unsalted butter
2/3 cup sugar
1/3 cup almonds
2 tablespoons cinnamon (preferably Ceylon)

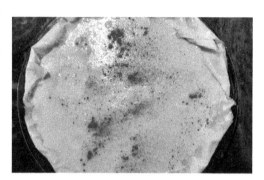

Melt the butter and set aside. In a pot add the milk, the sugar, the semolina, a drop of vanilla extract and a pinch of salt and turn the heat on at medium. Do not hesitate to add a pinch of salt to your desserts: it brings out all the flavors. Stir the cream with a good spatula, scraping the bottom of the pot until the mixture begins to thicken. Do *not* wait for it to become a thick cream. The cream is going to be baked later and it will thicken up again, so at this stage, we want a very thin consistency. Dip a spoon in the cream, take it out and run your finger through the back. If it leaves a trail, take the cream out of the heat immediately. In my kitchen that takes 7.5 minutes exactly, from the time I turn on the heat to when I take the cream off the heat. Let it cool slightly and then beat the two eggs and add them to the cream, stirring very well. Add the lemon zest also. Take a couple of tablespoons of butter and top the cream with it, so that it does not form a skin or place a plastic sheet directly on top of the cream.

Cut the almonds by hand in big chunks, roughly four to six pieces out of every almond. Mix 2/3 cup sugar, the almonds and 2 tablespoons cinnamon.

Turn the oven on at 400°F. Butter a 9 X 12 baking pan or a round pie dish. Open the phyllo package and lay it flat. Take two sheets, place them in the pan, with the ends covering and overhanging on the sides of the pan. Butter the top phyllo generously. Sprinkle three tablespoons of the sugar-almond-cinnamon mixture. Lay two more phyllo sheets, butter them generously and sprinkle some of the sugar mixture again. (Basically, this is one way to make baklava by repeating this process many times). Repeat it four or five times and then add the cream on top of the last phyllo (do not add sugar on the last phyllo). Turn the edges inwards around the top. Use the rest of the butter to brush the edge, and add a little cinnamon on the top of the cream. Bake until the cream is set and the bottom is golden brown. Serve warm.

When to make it: for a winter night dinner. Invite my husband, please.

Loukoumades

Loukoumades are the Greek donuts. Actually, they are more like donut holes and Greeks eat them with honey and walnuts. A popular topping with our students is sugar and cinnamon. They also top them with Merenda (the Greek version of Nutella), but I do not recommend it because it is highly addictive.

If you are a vegan you can make them with water. I just prefer the fuller taste milk gives them. This recipe yields about two dozen loukoumades.

2 cups milk 3.5% (500 ml)
1 package dry yeast
4 tablespoons sugar
3.5 cups flour (500 grams)
1 teaspoon salt

Vegetable oil for frying

You may use fresh milk or condensed. I do not use condensed milk very often, but in this recipe it works very well. If you do use condensed, use one cup milk and one cup water. Warm up the milk slightly (70-90°F) and then remove from the heat; add the sugar and yeast and mix well with a whisk. Add half of the flour and keep stirring until the mixture becomes smooth. Add the salt and the rest of the flour and mix well by hand. Cover with plastic wrap and let it rise for 30 minutes to two hours. Heat the frying pan to medium high. Do not choose the highest temperature setting or the loukoumades will burn. If you choose the lowest they will become too oily. Get a glass of water with a spoon to help you form the loukoumades.

Close your left hand in a loose fist with your thumb sticking up. Immerse your fist in the bowl of the dough, halfway, so that you can still see your thumb and index finger. Squeeze your fist. A perfect ball of dough will form between your thumb and index finger. Scoop it up with the wet spoon and carefully place it in the fryer. Squeeze your fist again and scoop a second loukouma. Continue with the rest of the dough, but do not overcrowd them in the fryer. Make sure you turn them so that they get a nice golden color all around. Make as many batches as you need. Take them out with a slotted ladle and place on a plate lined with kitchen paper to absorb any excess oil. While still hot, roll them in sugar and cinnamon or add honey on them.

When to make them: always?!?

Carrot Cake

A healthy, easy and very tasty cake. This is a big hit with our students who always get very excited when I make it, as the smell of cinnamon fills up not only the kitchen but the whole building. Very often, after I serve this cake, a student comes and gives me a tight, emotional hug; I guess the cinnamon smell brings out some nostalgic, childhood memories.

2 cups grated carrots; I prefer to make it with organic carrots because the taste is by far superior
1 cup white sugar
1 cup brown sugar
4 eggs
2 cups flour
1/2 teaspoon baking soda
1 teaspoon baking powder
1/2 teaspoon salt
1 tablespoon cinnamon
1/2 teaspoon vanilla
1 cup vegetable oil

Frosting
8 oz cream cheese
2 tablespoons unsalted butter, at room temperature
2 cups confectioners sugar
1 tablespoon cinnamon
A pinch of salt

Shred the carrots in a food processor or grate them by hand. In the end, the cake will be fluffier if the carrots are cut in a food processor because the shreds will be thinner. Do not overwork the food processor. We do not want to lose any juice from the carrots. Set aside. Turn the oven on at 380°F.

In a bowl mix the sugars with the eggs and beat until they start to become fluffy, around five minutes. In a separate bowl mix the flour with all the dry ingredients and add about 1/3 of the flour mixture to the egg mixture. Mix with the spatula until incorporated and then add half of the oil, mix again and add another 1/3 of the flour mixture. Mix and then add the rest of the oil. Mix and add the rest of the flour. Add the carrots and fold the mixture. Transfer to a 9 X 12 pan and bake in the oven for about an hour (55-60 minutes), until a knife comes out clean when inserted in the middle of the pan.

In the food processor add all frosting ingredients in room temperature and beat until well incorporated. You may want to add one more cup of confectioners sugar if you want your frosting to be thicker. I personally prefer a thinner, silkier frosting.

When to make it: when your "I hate healthy food" friends come over. You'll trick them into eating carrots.

Chocolate Mousse

This is a wonderful mousse that you can serve with strawberries or any other fruit and/or nuts. It is extremely tasty and has a silky texture. The problem with mousse is that it's made with raw eggs. Raw eggs will potentially develop salmonella. For salmonella to start developing, the eggs need to be at room temperature for 2 hours after they are cracked open. (Be careful that all the eggs you use for the mousse are intact). This means that you have to have the chocolate and butter melted before you crack the eggs and work quickly from then on. Do not crack the eggs and then go send a few emails and then come back to finish the dessert. Also, after I serve the mousse, I throw away any remains that have been outside the fridge for more than an hour, just to be on the safe side. There are almost never any leftovers, but we are just saying…

I love dark chocolate. I have experimented with this recipe and have reduced sugar to 0. It's bitter and wonderful. I have also reduced the cream to half and it is really good. Do not mess with the chocolate, butter, egg ratio.

18 ounces dark chocolate (500 grams)
2 sticks unsalted butter
Pinch of sea salt
5 eggs yolks (room temperature)
A drop of rum extract or 2 tablespoons dark rum (if you are not serving to children)
Vanilla extract
5 egg whites (room temperature)
1/2 cup sugar
2 cups heavy cream (400 ml)
1/2 cup sugar
1/2 teaspoon sea salt for topping

Place the chocolate and butter in a *bain marie* (page 12). You can alternatively melt them in a microwave. When all are melted add a pinch of sea salt. Salt has the aptitude/capacity to bring out the flavors of chocolate. In another bowl, crack the eggs and mix the egg yolks with the rum and the vanilla and place the egg whites in a mixer bowl. Start whipping the egg whites and slowly add 1/2 cup sugar. Do not overbeat the meringue, It needs to be a soft peak meringue. When you lift the mixer whisk, the peak should lean over. Add the melted chocolate to the egg yolks and as soon as the meringue is ready add it to the mixture as well. Fold a few tablespoons of the meringue in the chocolate mixture at first to loosen up the mixture, and then fold in the rest. Your movements should be slow and gentle, folding from top to bottom with your right hand while at the same time turning the bowl counterclockwise with your left hand. When you have incorporated the meringue (do not worry if it is not completely incorporated at this point) quickly place the mousse in the freezer for a few minutes. (Do not keep it in the freezer for more than ten minutes). We want the temperature to drop, but we do not want the mousse to freeze. Very quickly beat the heavy cream with the rest of the sugar to a nice soft cream. Again, we want soft peaks. We do not want stiff peaks for either the meringue or the cream because that will stiffen up the mouse too much and the texture will not be pleasant. Take the mousse out of the freezer and incorporate the cream into the mousse with the same soft movements. This time mix thoroughly until there are no white spots left. If you prefer dark chocolate, beat up less heavy cream and sugar. Transfer to a nice crystal bowl and place it in the refrigerator for at least two hours to set. Just before you serve, take a generous pinch of sea salt between your fingers, crushing any big flakes and sprinkle on top of the mousse. It's extremely pleasant to eat chocolate mousse with salt flakes. Serve with strawberries or grapes and/or nuts.

You're welcome.

Upside Down Apple Cake with Creme Anglaise

4 tablespoons melted unsalted butter
1/2 cup sugar
2 teaspoons cinnamon
4 apples

2 eggs
1 cup sugar
1 stick unsalted butter at room temperature
2 cups flour
2 teaspoons baking powder
1 teaspoon cinnamon
Vanilla extract
Salt
3/4 cup whole milk

Crème Anglaise (vanilla sauce)
1 cup whole milk
1 cup cream
1/2 cup sugar
1/2 vanilla bean
4 egg yolks
1 tablespoon cornstarch

Butter a 9 X 12 pan and line it with parchment paper. The parchment paper will help us in unmolding the cake and will also facilitate the creation of a nice crust on the top. Melt 4 tablespoons butter. Carefully pour the butter on the parchment paper and then add the sugar and the cinnamon, evenly. Peel the apples and remove the seeds. Slice the apples into disks and arrange the most beautiful pieces as the first layer. Proceed with cutting all the apples and layering them in the pan. If you like cinnamon add an extra teaspoon.
Turn the oven on at 425 °F. This is purposely a bit higher than what we choose for most cakes because we want to create a nice caramelized bottom. Mix together the flour, the baking powder, the cinnamon and the salt. In a mixer bowl beat one stick of butter (room temperature) with one cup sugar and the vanilla until they turn pale yellow. Add the two eggs and mix some more. Turn the mixer off and add 1/3 of the flour mixture and start mixing with a rubber spatula. Add some milk, then flour, then milk again and end with the rest of the flour. Pour the batter over the apples. Tap the pan a couple of times from the bottom to release any trapped air and place it in the oven. After about 20 minutes, lower the heat to 400 °F. Bake for a total of 45-50 minutes until, when inserting a knife, it comes out clean. When ready, take out of the oven. Let it cool for 5 minutes and then place a nice platter on the pan and turn it upside down. Carefully remove the parchment paper. Ideally, serve hot with vanilla ice cream or Crème Anglaise.

Crème Anglaise. It is better if you make it one day in advance to let the flavors infuse.

In a heavy pot combine the milk, the cream and the sugar. With a sharp knife cut a vanilla bean in half (store the other half in an airtight container or in a jar with sugar) split the half bean lengthwise and scrape out the vanilla seeds. Add the seeds and bean to the milk. Turn the heat on at medium. Do not stir the sugar to dissolve; it is covering the bottom of the pot, protecting the milk from burning. In another bowl add the egg yolks and the cornstarch and mix well. When the milk starts to steam, transfer the hot milk, all at once to the egg mixture while simultaneously whisking the egg mixture vigorously. Now return the milk-egg mixture to the pot, turn the heat down to low and continue stirring constantly with a whisk. As soon as the mixture bubbles up, take it off the heat immediately. Very quickly transfer through a sieve to a clean bowl to stop the cooking and place the bowl in another bowl filled with ice water. In the unfortunate event that your cream does curdle up, whisk it with an electric hand mixer and pass it through a sieve, one more time. Cover with plastic wrap directly on the surface of the cream to avoid any skin from forming. It's better to serve the cream cold on the hot apple pie, but I have served both warm and nobody complained.

Creamy Apple pie

Basic Crust
1.5 cup flour
1 tablespoon vinegar
1/2 teaspoon salt
1/2 cup cold unsalted butter
2 tablespoons cold milk
Extra butter for the pan

Filling
3 apples
2 cups sugar
2 teaspoons cinnamon
6 tablespoons cornstarch
A pinch of salt
Vanilla
2 cups cream

Add the flour, the vinegar, the salt and the cold butter in a food processor and pulse until all the butter is incorporated. Add two tablespoons of cold milk and pulse again. If your mixture is dry you might need to add a bit more milk. Pulse again until the dough turns into a ball. Remove immediately, form it into a ball, flatten it (to facilitate the rolling into a pie crust later), wrap it up in plastic wrap, and place in the fridge for, at least, thirty minutes.

Preheat the oven to 375°F. Take the dough out of the fridge, place it between two parchment papers and roll it out. Place the rolled dough in a buttered 8 X 10 rectangular pan (a 9 X 12 pan would also work), prick it several times with a fork and bake for about 10 minutes.

In the meantime, peel the apples and core them. With a mandoline cut the apples in thin (less than 1/4 of an inch thick) slices. Try to stack them up neatly as they fall off the mandoline.

In a clean bowl combine the dry ingredients, add the cream and whisk.

Take the pie crust out of the oven. Arrange the apples on the pie crust as neatly as possible. Pour the cream mixture on top of the apples and return to the oven. Bake for 50-55 minutes until the cream is set.

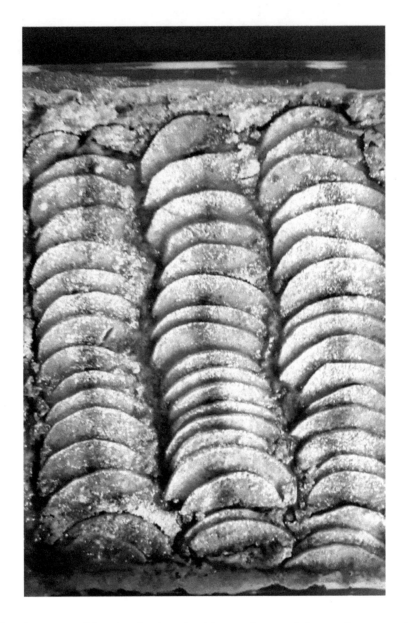

When to make it: when your friend, who has just been dumped, is coming over. It is the ultimate consolation dessert. Eat some vanilla ice-cream, too!

Greek Cheese pie

This is not really a typical Greek dessert, but I have combined a couple of Greek desserts, added some red fruit on top, and ended up with this gem.

The difficulty with this recipe is that two of the ingredients are unique. *Anthotyro* cheese and mastic. Both can be found in specialty shops or on several websites. You can substitute anthotyro with ricotta cheese, but ricotta has more moisture, so you need to add two tablespoons more flour in the filling. Mastic is a unique Greek product. It is sap collected from trees only on the island of Chios. It is a therapeutic super ingredient (fights stomach ulcers, teeth decay and cholesterol, to name a few) and has a unique flavor, like an evergreen aroma. Be very careful when you add mastic, as too much of it will turn the cream bitter. You can substitute it with orange zest and cinnamon, although it is not the same flavor. Having said that, I strongly suggest that you try to find both anthotyro and mastic as the taste of this unique cheesecake is delicate and distinguished. Also, anthotyro is a low fat cheese!

Crust
3 cups flour
2 tablespoons sugar
1/2 teaspoon salt
1.5 stick butter
6 tablespoons milk
1 egg
Butter for the pan
Filling
1 pound Greek cheese anthotyro
2 cups sugar
1 egg
2/3 cup flour
1 teaspoon baking powder
Vanilla
5-6 pearls crushed mastic or
orange zest plus cinnamon
1.5 cup frozen berries. I get a mixture of strawberries, raspberries and blueberries. (Let them thaw on a kitchen paper to get rid of moisture)

In a food processor mix the flour, salt, sugar and very briefly the butter (cut the butter in cubes first). Just pulse a few times until big lumps are created. Remove a cup of this flour-butter mixture, cover it up, and set aside. Add one egg and 4 tablespoons milk in the processor and pulse again until one big ball of dough forms. (It might need one more tablespoon of milk). Be very careful not to overwork your dough. Form your dough into a ball and flatten it in a disc. Cover in plastic wrap and refrigerate for at least 30 minutes.

Turn the oven on to 400 °F. In a food processor add the cheese, the sugar, the egg and the mastic or zest of an orange with 1 teaspoon of cinnamon. Work the food processor until you have a smooth cream. Add the flour, the baking powder, the vanilla and mix until well incorporated.

Take the dough out of the refrigerator. Roll the crust (you might need to dust with flour) and place it on a buttered 9-inch diameter pie shell. Add the cream and level the top. Place the berries on top of the cream as evenly as possible. Finally, spread the flour-butter mixture you removed from the pie crust dough earlier. Bake for 50-55 minutes or until golden brown and set.

When to make it: when you are invited to your Greek friend's home. You'll mess up with their minds because the flavors are extremely Greek, but the combination is not.

Orange soufflé

3 tablespoons unsalted butter
4 tablespoons flour
1.5 cup milk
1 cup freshly squeezed orange juice
Zest of 2 oranges
1/4 cup sugar
1 teaspoon salt
3 egg yolks
3 egg whites
1/2 cup sugar
Butter and sugar for the pan

Ganache (optional)
250 ml of heavy cream
8 ounces dark chocolate finely chopped
1/4 teaspoon salt
Vanilla

In a heavy saucepan over medium heat melt the butter. Add the flour and cook for two minutes until you get a thick paste. Gradually add the milk while whisking constantly. Add the orange juice and zest and keep whisking. It should be a thick sauce by now. Turn the heat off and add the salt, 1/4 cup sugar, and taste. It should have a wonderful and strong orange flavor. (Remember that you are adding 1/2 cup sugar with the meringue to the mixture later). If not, add more orange juice and/or salt. If the sauce is too thick but the orange taste is strong, add half a cup of milk.

Turn the oven on at 370°F and butter a soufflé baking dish. If you are using ramekins, butter them and turn the oven to 350°F. Sprinkle with sugar the buttered dish.

Add the three egg yolks to the orange mixture and start whisking the egg whites with a mixer. Gradually add the sugar. Beat the meringue (egg whites with sugar) until the mixer whisk leaves a trail on the meringue and soft peaks are formed when you lift it up. Incorporate the meringue to the orange mixture by folding gently with a spatula. Your movement should be soft and slow and steady. Fold the mixture by moving your right hand from top to bottom, while at the same time turning the bowl counterclockwise with your left hand. Do not overwork the mixture or it will lose some of the fluffiness. Transfer the orange mixture to the baking pan or ramekins and bake for 50 minutes if you have one big pan, 30-35 if you have ramekins. Serve with powdered sugar or Ganache.

Ganache: In a heavy saucepan heat up the cream over very low heat. When steam starts to emerge, turn the heat off and pour the cream over the chopped chocolate that you have placed in a bowl. Let it stand for 3-4 minutes and then start mixing gently with a whisk until all chocolate is melted. Add the salt and vanilla. It will become a wonderful, silky sauce that you can use with the orange soufflé. You can also use it as a dip for strawberries or bananas, or after it has cooled down and thickened, as a spread. It is simply delicious.

When to make it: when you want to go on an adventure and experience something new and exotic but also don't want to leave the house.

Greek orange cake

This is a lovely dessert/cake. Because phyllo dough is used instead of flour, the texture of the cake is unique; it almost feels like there is yeast in it. Along with the interesting texture, cinnamon and orange flavors hit your mouth in waves. It is really good. We serve it with either vanilla ice cream or Greek yogurt, and it is good both ways. The only catch with this cake is that you have to do some preparation the day before. Otherwise, it is quite easy. This recipe is for 12-15 people.

Syrup
2 cups sugar
1 cup water
1 cup freshly squeezed orange juice
1 cinnamon stick (if you don't have it, just add 1 teaspoon of cinnamon)
Cake
4 whole medium oranges
4 tablespoons sugar
1 package of phyllo dough
6 eggs
1 cup sugar
12 ounces Greek yogurt (2% or more)
1 cup olive oil (you could substitute half or all with melted, unsalted butter)
1 cup freshly squeezed orange juice
Zest of one orange
A pinch of salt
1/2 teaspoon vanilla
2 teaspoons cinnamon
1 teaspoon baking soda
2 teaspoons baking powder
2 tablespoons olive oil for the pan

The day before: Take the package of phyllo dough out of the fridge or freezer and let it warm up to room temperature. Open the package and slice the rolled dough with a sharp knife (as you would cut cinnamon rolls). Arrange the phyllo strips loosely on a cookie sheet. Cover them with kitchen paper or a towel and let them dry overnight.

In a small pot place two oranges with water covering them completely and bring to a boil. We want to boil them until tender, around 20-25 minutes. Slice the remaining two oranges as evenly as possible and add them to another pot along with one cup of water and 4 tablespoons sugar and bring to a boil over very low heat. When the water is almost all evaporated, turn the heat off and transfer the oranges to a plate. We will use them for decoration. These three preparations are basically the most time consuming.

On the following day.

In a pot add all the syrup ingredients and boil them for five minutes. Take off the heat and let the syrup cool completely.

Turn the oven on at 400°F. Cut the boiled oranges in half and remove any seeds. Place them in a food processor, peels and flesh, and pulse until completely pureed. In the standing mixer bowl add the eggs and the sugar and beat for 3-4 minutes. Add the rest of the ingredients along with the pureed orange and mix with a spatula until all are incorporated. Sprinkle a 10 X 16 inch pan with two tablespoons of olive oil. Place in it the dried phyllo dough, making sure you break any large chunks. Evenly spread the batter and tap the pan from the bottom, so that any trapped air is released. Make sure all the phyllo strips are immersed in the batter. Let the unbaked dessert sit for ten minutes so that the phyllo absorbs the liquid, tap again and place it in the oven. Bake until golden brown, 50 to 55 minutes. Make sure that the color is deep, so that the flavors are intense. Take the cake out of the oven and prick the surface of the cake with a fork. Very carefully add the syrup making sure that you moisten all the surface of the cake. Place the decorative oranges on top and serve with either vanilla ice cream or Greek yogurt.

Banana Bread

What would be a good reason for a banana bread recipe to be included in a Greek cookbook? Greek Yogurt! We already know that Greek yogurt makes everything taste better, right? Well, we use Greek yogurt in the banana bread and the result is amazing. A juicy cake with substance and taste!

2 sticks unsalted butter at room temperature
1.5 cup sugar plus 2 tablespoons for the pan
3 eggs
1 cup Greek yogurt 2% or more
1/2 cup heavy cream
1.5 cup mashed bananas
4 cups flour
1 teaspoon baking soda
1 teaspoon baking powder
A pinch of salt
2 tablespoons cinnamon
1/8 teaspoon grated clove

Turn the oven on at 380°F. Butter a Bundt cake pan and sprinkle it with sugar.
In the mixer whisk together the butter and the sugar until fluffy. Add the eggs, one at a time. Turn the mixer on low and add the yogurt, the cream and the bananas and mix until the batter is smooth. Turn the mixer off. Mix the flour with all the dry ingredients and add the flour mixture to the batter, mixing with a spatula now. When all ingredients are incorporated, transfer to the buttered cake form and bake for 50-55 minutes or until a knife comes out clean when inserted in the cake. Serve warm, dressed with powdered sugar and a dollop of butter.

When to make it: on a Saturday winter morning, when you start planning your next summer vacation in Greece.

Tiramisu

This Italian masterpiece will become a favorite with your friends and family. Oh, the compliments I have gotten for this dessert!
I used to make Tiramisu with mascarpone until one time there was a shortage of it in the supermarket and I reluctantly made it with the much cheaper cream cheese. To my surprise, it turned out even better!

2 cups strong brewed coffee (French Roast works well)
2 tablespoons dark rum or a drop of rum extract if you are serving children
1 package store bought ladyfingers (you will need 10 ounces for a 9 X 12 pan)

6 egg yolks
1 cup sugar
1 gelatin sheet (2 grams) or one teaspoon gelatin powder
1 cup cream
3 ounces cream cheese
A pinch of salt
3 tablespoons unsweetened organic cocoa powder

Make the coffee and add the rum or rum extract and set aside to cool.
Place the gelatin sheet in another bowl with cold water to soak (see page 13). If you are in the U.S., you will find gelatin powder easier than gelatin sheets. I think (check the instructions on your box) the conversion rate is one gelatin sheet equals one teaspoon.
In a small pot add some water and bring to a boil. In a metallic bowl add the egg yolks and the sugar. Place the metallic bowl on top of the boiling pot, in a *bain marie* (page 12) and with a hand electric mixer, start beating up the egg yolks and sugar. Beat for 3.5 to 4 minutes, or until the mixture turns lighter in color and thicker in texture; it should be warm if you touch it. Turn the mixer off and take the bowl off the heat. Take the gelatin sheet out of the water and squeeze it well. Add the gelatin sheet or gelatin powder to the egg mixture and turn the mixer on again for half a minute until you cannot see any lumps from the gelatin. Set aside. Place the cream and cream cheese in another bowl and beat with the mixer until soft peaks form. With a spatula fold the cream into the egg mixture. Add salt and taste. The salt should counterbalance the sweetness of the cream. I usually add two or three pinches of salt. Set aside.
In a 9 X 12 inch pan or serving dish, start layering the ladyfingers, after you dip each one in the coffee for 3-4 seconds. Arrange tightly side by side. Add half of the cream mixture and repeat with the second layer of ladyfingers. Add the rest of the cream and cover with plastic wrap. Leave in the fridge for at least five hours before you serve, or preferably overnight. Just before you serve, dress the tiramisu with a generous amount of unsweetened cocoa, by sprinkling it through a strainer. The bitter cocoa powder is essential in balancing the flavors.

In the Tiramisu of the picture, I used eggs from a home farm, where the chickens are fed corn. You can see how orange the cream is because of how orange the yolks were. It will be a lot whiter if made with store bought eggs, but just as tasty.

When to make it: every time you remember your vacation in Italy.

Clafoutis

This is one of the most fun desserts. It is flan with cherries, and maybe chocolate (don' t tell your French friends that) topped with burned sugar. Really exciting!

There is a big debate in France (one of the reasons I love France is how serious the debates over food are) about whether the cherries should be left with the pits or not. French grandmas never make their Clafoutis without the pits in the cherries. Frankly, after making this dessert for many years without the pits, I was convinced to try it with the pits this spring for the first time and I have to admit that it was by far superior. So, use the cherries with the pits.

1 stick unsalted butter at room temperature
3 eggs
1 1/8 cup flour (5 oz)
Vanilla
A pinch of salt
2/3 cup sugar (3 oz)
1 cup warm milk (220 ml)
2 cups whole cherries or 10oz (you can use canned if not in season)
4 oz dark chocolate (this is not in the original French recipe)
Butter and sugar for the pan
2-3 tablespoons brown sugar for the topping

Beat the butter (at room temperature) with the eggs and the flour until the mixture starts to become lighter in color. Add the vanilla and a pinch of salt along with half the sugar. Turn the mixer off and add the rest of the sugar and warm milk. Mix with a spatula until well incorporated. It will be a very runny mixture. Turn the oven on at 380°F. Butter a 9 inch pie dish. Sprinkle the pan with sugar generously and then shake off any loose sugar. Place the cherries in the pie dish evenly. Cut the chocolate into small squares and add the chocolate pieces with the cherries. Very carefully pour the batter on top and transfer to the oven. Bake until set and lightly golden, 35-40 minutes. Sprinkle with the brown sugar and burn the top with a torch, if you have one. The sugar will caramelize filling the house with the irresistible aroma of caramel. If you don't have a torch, turn the broiler in your oven on. Place the dessert under the broiler at the middle rack but do not leave it unattended. A good tip when using the broiler is to open the oven door briefly every ninety seconds to allow humidity to escape, thus facilitating the caramelization of the sugar. Take it off as soon as the sugar melts after 3 or 4 minutes.

When to make it: when you have friends with children over. If they do not burn your house down, you will all have a lot of fun caramelizing the sugar.

CONTENTS

After leaving Greece I was dying for one of Natasa's recipes. Fortunately, she was willing to lend me her lemon chicken and potatoes recipe and it was exactly how I remembered it. It was juicy with just the right amount of zest. Any recipe from this chef is guaranteed to be delicious.   *LilyAnne Witt, student in Greece in the Spring semester of 2020*

Natasa's recipes are so beloved that they have made their way to our table during the holiday season. Her pepper jelly was the only non-negotiable item in our Christmas Eve dinner! Her lemon chicken and potatoes are a great way to get our family gathered around the table, and her fried zucchini is always a crowd favorite!   *Hope Walker, Spring 2019*

I studied abroad in Greece and ate exclusively Nastasa's cooking for 3 months and every bite was by far the best bite I had ever experienced! I spent almost all of my free time in her kitchen learning to cook like her. The pastisio is my absolute favorite!! Thanks to Natasa, I am a more creative and knowledgeable cook for my family and friends, and I always leave the social event with an empty dish!   *Miranda Lynn Farthing, Spring 2015*

I made Natasa's pork with raisins dish for classmates and they all loved it! It was easy to make and was so delicious! It made me feel like I was back in Greece!
          Tony Sharp, Studies Nutrition & Dietetics, Spring 2018

I have carried back home with me many things that I have learned from Natasa. One of my personal favorites is her steamed potatoes. I make them frequently for my friends and family. Even though I am no longer in Greece, I still try to learn from Natasa and frequently text her and ask for recipes or how to do something and she is always a big help. Her recipes are the best of the best and they will not let you down. She will teach you everything you need to know about cooking!   *Mark Randall Potter, Summer 2019*

One day (Na)Tasa was making tiramisu as a dessert, and I remember I was so mad because I was going into Athens that day (and I would miss dessert). So later that night, I sneaked into the kitchen when everyone was sleeping and ate so much tiramisu. Tiramisu has never tasted that good, even when I was in Italy. I made this recipe and it was a close second to Tasa's! Tasa, you rock!   *Cassie Copeland, Spring 2019*

CPSIA information can be obtained
at www.ICGtesting.com
Printed in the USA
BVHW020113191120
593636BV00003B/15